OREGON
COAST
HIKES

OREGON COAST HIKES

By Paul M. Williams
Photographs by Bob and Ira Spring

THE MOUNTAINEERS • SEATTLE

The Mountaineers: Organized 1906
". . . to explore, study, preserve and enjoy
the natural beauty of the Northwest."

Safety is an important concern in all outdoor activities. No guidebook can alert you to every hazard or anticipate the limitations of every reader, so the descriptions in this book are not representations that a particular trip is safe for your party. When you take a trip, you assume responsibility for your own safety. Some of the trips described in this book may require you to do no more than look both ways before crossing the street; on others, more attention to safety may be required due to terrain, traffic, weather, the capabilities of your party, or other factors. Keeping informed on current conditions and exercising common sense are the keys to a safe, enjoyable outing.

Published by
The Mountaineers
306 Second Avenue West, Seattle, Washington 98119

Published simultaneously in Canada by
Douglas & McIntyre Ltd.
1615 Venables St.
Vancouver, B.C. V5L 2H1

Manufactured in the United States of America

Edited by Maureen A. Zimmerman
Designed by Constance Bollen
Maps by Tom Kirkendall
Photos by Bob and Ira Spring
Cover photo: Clam digging on the Oregon coast
Frontispiece: Neahkahnie Beach from side of Neahkahnie Mountain

Library of Congress Cataloging in Publication Data
Williams, Paul, 1925-
    Oregon coast hikes.

    Includes index.
    1. Hiking–Oregon–Guide-books. 2. Oregon–
Description and travel–1981–   –Guide-books.
I. Spring, Bob, 1918–   . II. Spring, Ira.
III. Title.
GV199.42.O7W55   1985   917.95   85-5055
ISBN 0-89886-105-5

0 9 8 7
5 4 3

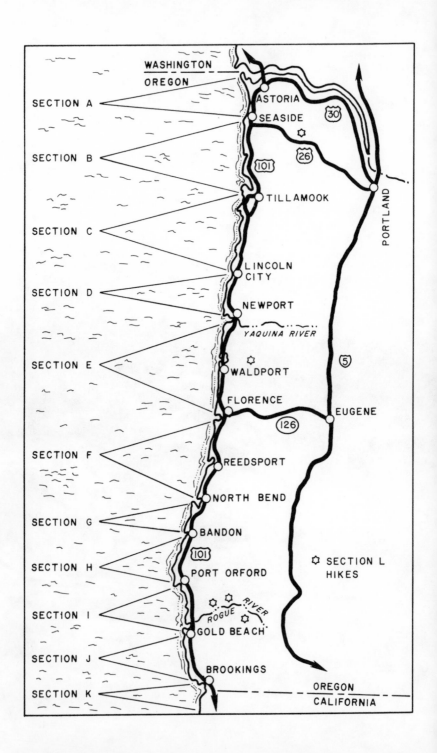

CONTENTS

Cannon Beach from Ecola State Park

PREFACE

This is a guidebook for all hikers, young and old – for the most athletic hikers as well as those who like to poke along looking into tidal pools and investigating the treasures the ocean casts ashore. The Oregon coast comprises over 350 miles of sandy beaches, rugged headlands, and some of the most famous marine views in the country. There are a number of substantial rivers and estuaries to cross or find a way around, and some of the headlands involve long detours.

Most of the 65 trips described in this guide are designed to be hiked in a day, and the majority are suitable for children. The few exceptions will be noted in the text.

It is possible through strenuous effort to cover several hikes in one day, but I don't advise it. The price, even with light packs and feet toughened by years of hiking, is hot spots and blisters. But more to the point, the traveler passes interesting places where it is worthwhile to linger and spend a little time photographing and enjoying the passing scenery. For example, the 16-odd miles from the south jetty of the Columbia River to Gearhart can be done in one day, but you will arrive at Gearhart with sore feet and will have missed an opportunity to inspect an old coastal fort. And you will have to roar by the wreck of the *Peter Iredale*, certainly a place to stop and linger. This is a trip that should be hiked in two days.

Most people will never have the time to hike the whole Oregon coast. However, they will find this guidebook useful for locating the most appealing beaches and trails to hike. Optional routes are often suggested for hikers interested in walking as much of the beach as possible. One day, the Oregon Coast Trail system may be completed (see Section A introduction).

This book is written from north to south, mainly because that is the way we hiked it. Whether you actually hike north or south in a particular section will depend on your preference, taking into account prevailing wind, ease of access, and other considerations.

The hikes in this book are not necessarily wilderness experiences. On a map the Oregon coast looks very populated, and much of it is. However, there are some wilderness beaches where the highway is miles inland, where houses cannot be seen, and where one may hike all day without meeting another person. When civilization does overlook the beach there often are intriguing small towns to shop in and the constant, changing panorama of summer homes with their unusual architecture.

One of the most marvelous things about the Oregon coast is that it's as much, if not more, fun to walk in winter as in summer. When we are locked

Deer at Cape Arago State Park

out of the mountains by winter or just tired of snow and skiing, the Oregon beaches provide a welcome change of scene.

Roads, access routes and river courses may change. I returned six months later and found the so-called wilderness termination of one hike occupied by a mobile home. I found the mouth of the Elk River had been changed by winter storms so that it entered an old channel and actually exited into the ocean a mile north of what is shown on a 15-year-old map. New trails are being built. A new subdivision, by creating easier access, may open previously private lands to public use. There are a number of beaches that simply go off into the distance to dead-end against a cliff. It is impossible for me to know all the "secret" trails that can be used to gain access along the way.

I must acknowledge the contributions of an informal group of friends who accompanied me on many of these hikes. They are Bill and Lucy Dougal, Ann Hall, Paul Stocklin, Bill Hanson, and many others over many trips. More importantly, I acknowledge the contribution of my wife of more than thirty years. Pat dropped me at many a beach and, after driving to the other end, waited without complaint while I had the fun of cruising along with nature.

I have, however, immensely enjoyed the process of creating this book, and I hope that if new trails are found or conditions change for better or for worse, you will drop me a line. I hope you will enjoy using this book as much as I've enjoyed producing it.

Paul M. Williams
143 Fifth Avenue North
Edmonds, WA 98020

WHAT YOU'LL NEED TO KNOW

By and large the Oregon beaches consist of smooth, compacted sand providing easy walking, with only occasional difficult sections of soft sand or loose, smooth rock.

The beaches are broken by points and rocky headlands which must be rounded at low tide or crossed by trails that have existed for hundreds of years. Originally, when the beaches were the only roadways, the headland trails were foot-beaten paths first used by Indians and then by white settlers. Fortunately, most of the headlands are now Oregon State parks where the trails have been preserved. A case in point is the trail over Tillamook Head in Ecola State Park, which follows the Indian trail described by Lewis and Clark. A little farther south, the excellent trail through Oswald West State Park from Arch Cape over Cape Falcon and down to Manzanita was formerly a pioneer road.

Many of the headlands and slopes behind the beaches are covered with a dense impenetrable brush, making it imperative that hikers find the established trails.

Coping With The Environment

Since U.S. 101 runs close behind the beach for much of the way, there is generally ready access to and from the highway. However, enough wilderness is involved that a hiker should carry a day pack and be prepared to cope with wind, changing weather, or unexpected delays.

WIND

Fifteen- to 30-mile-per-hour winds are common along the Oregon coast. The trick is to be flexible and plan the day's hike with the wind at your back and not wear yourself out bucking it. However, predicting the wind is difficult. There are as many theories as there are "experts." My "expert" theory is that Newport is the turning point for the prevailing winds. Above Newport the wind generally comes from the south, while from Newport to the California border the wind is from the north. However, other experienced hikers claim that except for the southwest storms most of the wind comes from the northwest. Listen to the "experts," but the best advice is to tune into the weather reports on the radio and plan the day's hike accordingly.

WEATHER

My unscientific opinion, based on years of hiking, is that the coast itself has much better weather than the immediate interior. I have often found the weather right beside the ocean considerably better than a mile or two inland. Clouds tend to scoot over the beach, leaving only a few drops of rain, and then dump their load of moisture when they are forced to rise over coastal hills.

My favorite time to hike the beach is in the winter. One must be more alert to changes in the weather, for storms roll in more frequently and with greater intensity than in the summer. In the winter there are days of gale-force winds and driving rain, when the best way to see the ocean may be from a motel window. Between storms, you can enjoy some of the best hiking of the year. For winter also brings less fog and some of the coast's clearest days. At Florence my companions and I once watched children playing in the surf on a balmy New Year's Day that felt more like August than January.

In the winter the surf is higher and more exciting than in the summer. The waves carry ashore mounds of sea foam, many treasures to pick over, and even an occasional glass float. Another bonus is the absence of people. Frequently it is possible to breeze down an empty beach on a cool, clear, sunny day with no one in sight except one's own group. The beach may be lined with houses whose windows are empty eyes, but when you meet someone there is always a cheerful greeting because all know how fortunate the select few are to be out in that big beautiful world.

TIDES

An amazing transformation takes place with the coming of the high tide. The smooth walkable sand is covered with water; all that is left to hike on is soft sand and driftwood. Many of the headlands that can be walked around at low tide become impassable at high tide, forcing you to find another way or wait for the tide to go out. A thirty-minute hike at low tide may take several tiring hours when the tide is in.

It is important to obtain a tide table, available at local sporting goods stores. Some tides are much lower than others. It is a good idea to plan a hike during the three or four times a year when a minus tide occurs. In general, the lower the low tide the higher the accompanying high tide. So, plan a hike to take advantage of the low tides and beware of incoming tides that may trap you against an unclimbable cliff. Since variations occur in tide heights between winter and summer, it is best to study the tide table to get a feeling for the sequences.

STREAM CROSSINGS

The text points out which streams can normally be crossed rather easily, but storms and high tides can cause unexpected problems. As a general rule, if the water is more than knee deep don't attempt to cross any stream – IT IS TOO DANGEROUS. You may find a bridge of driftwood. If not, try to find another way around. Since U.S. 101 is generally nearby, the best answer – where possible – is to follow the stream to the highway and cross by bridge. If this is not practical, you can wait for the stream level to drop (high water caused by a storm normally runs off in about 12 hours) or for low tide, when the stream may fan out and become shallower. Or you may have to go back the way you came.

Cape Arago from Seven Devils Wayside

BIG WAVES

Old-timers warn of big "sleeper" waves, a series of waves that are bigger than the rest and sweep high up the beach. These are especially dangerous on jetties or rocky headlands where there is no place to escape. While the waves are not common, it is well to heed the old-timers' advice and keep a wary eye on the ocean.

What to Take

Go prepared with basic equipment. On one occasion in February, my wife, a friend and I walked north on the wilderness beach from Cape Blanco for 12½ miles toward Bandon. A strong northward storm propelled us along. Everything went fine until we came to Fourmile Creek, a small stream that normally we could wade across in ankle-deep water–but this time the creek looked like the Columbia River. Our 12½-mile hike now turned into a 25-mile hike, and–even worse–the return trip was into the storm. A flashlight became essential, extra food was desirable, and rain gear became imperative. While normally the highway is accessible for ready escape, this time there was no way to reach it. What started as a moderate hike turned into an exhausting survival trek.

CLOTHING

Wool clothing is recommended, since wool retains a substantial quantity of heat even when wet. A wool ski hat is most desirable. Good rain gear is imperative. Some of us use the latest water-repellent jackets and pants; others simply use the old heavy yellow slicker outfits. Inexpensive rain pants are a must in rain.

TEN ESSENTIALS

Carry a day pack with the "ten essentials"—map; compass (you may be trying to escape off a headland to the· highway); matches in a waterproof container; some sort of fire starter, such as candles; a flashlight and extra batteries (why do the batteries wear out just when they are needed the most?); a small first aid kit (include tape for blisters and hot spots); sunglasses; a pocket knife; extra clothing; and extra food. You may also want to bring a camera, binoculars, and a bird book—nonessentials but desirable.

FOOTWEAR

During the winter, when it's wet, my hiking companions and I use rubber boots—the only practical footwear. Get them large enough for several pairs of socks. Felt insoles make the walking much softer. The best type of rubber boot is one that laces all the way to the toe, instead of the kind with just three

Great blue heron tracks

or four laces at the top. The latter boot becomes impossible to put on or take off when wet. Rubber boots will allow the traveler to go through mud puddles and small streams, run around a tidal point when the water is out (you hope), and walk through small pools.

If there is an accident and your boots become filled with water, wring out your socks and put them back on. It is better to have wet but warm feet.

In the summer, on sandy beaches with only an occasional small stream to cross, jogging shoes are acceptable. Leather boots are certainly usable but they are heavier than jogging shoes and don't retain the heat in the event of wetness like rubber boots do. However, leather boots are recommended for forest and river trails.

Methods of Travel

You'll need to choose a method of transportation to the starting point of each hike and to decide how to return from the stopping point. Also, you may require a camping spot or a motel room for an overnight stay.

BY CAR OR BUS

Your best bet is to set up a shuttle using two motor vehicles. First, estimate the distance you will travel that day; then drop one car off at your destination; finally, drive back to the beginning of the hike and park.

With only one vehicle there are several options. First, you can simply retrace your steps. Surprisingly, the views on the return trip will look so different it will be almost like hiking a different beach. Another possibility is to find a young person in a gas station who can be hired to transport you in his car for $5 to $10. Have him follow you to a parking spot at the trail's end and then transport you to the beginning point. Still another alternative, though less desirable, is to simply hike the beach and then endeavor to find someone available for transportation back. Finally, you can travel with someone who would rather spend the day sightseeing or fishing and would be happy to drop you off and pick you up at the end of the hike.

HITCHHIKING IS NOT RECOMMENDED. First, it's dangerous; second, after coming off the beach in old clothes, sweaty and tired, your chances of being transported are rather slim.

It is also possible to travel up and down the coast by common carrier bus. At present buses head north and south in the morning, afternoon, and late evening. They stop only at scheduled "flag stops," usually in towns—a great limitation on bus travel. A charitable driver might drop you off at a nonscheduled stop, but don't count on it. It is worthwhile to call or stop in at a bus depot for the latest schedule.

CROSSING PRIVATE PROPERTY

There is a simple basic rule regarding private property—DON'T TRESPASS. No property owner wants a parade of people coming by his or her house. Probably there is legal access onto the beach nearby. If you miss the legal access and need to cross someone's property, simply go up and ask permission.

In all probability it will be granted, and you will have made a friend who will be a good source of information about local travel problems.

CAMPING AND BACKPACKING

Because of the scarcity of camping spots, backpacking simply isn't practical along most of the Oregon coast. There are few places where one can put up a tent out of sight of a house or out of the view of a beach hiker.

There has been talk of a law prohibiting any beach camping in Oregon. Hopefully this will remain just talk. Currently, camping on the beach in the immediate vicinity of a state park or within sight of a house is prohibited. It is therefore very difficult to find a decent beach campsite; finding one with water is almost impossible. Perhaps, as the Oregon Coast Trail (see Section A introduction) is extended, this will change. Right now there are, as noted in the list on page 203, some wilderness stretches, such as Blacklock Point, where camping is a joy. Generally, beach fires are discouraged by the State of Oregon; building a fire in driftwood is prohibited.

Backpackers will need a rainproof tent and a small, portable stove for boiling drinking water and cooking. Except for that which comes from a tap, there isn't any safe water along the Oregon coast. There are just too many people and animals for the natural water to be safe. A number of chemical purifiers and microporous filters are currently available, but my preference is to boil the water at least 10 minutes. A parasite called "giardia" presents a real danger: it induces disabling diarrhea. Those who have had it will go to extreme lengths to avoid a repetition of the illness.

Camping facilities in numerous county parks, state parks, and private campgrounds are noted in the text. However, during the summer it may be difficult to find a vacant spot, and during the off-season many are closed. Oregon State parks, quite reasonably, charge out-of-state users a surcharge over their regular rates.

MOTELS

Tent camping is great. I love hearing the sounds of night and the crashing surf, but when there is no place to pitch a tent or the weather is bad, I do prefer to have my bivouac with a hot shower and a warm bed. After spending enough nights huddled under a tree, I now do my roughing-it in a motel.

Motels range from plush holiday resorts to simple accommodations that are 40 to 60 years old. The latter are, of course, considerably cheaper and have their own rustic attractiveness. Generally, any motel adjacent to the beach will probably be filled during the summer and on holiday weekends. Accordingly, it is best to call ahead and make reservations. However, away from the beach in towns and alongside the highway, motel rooms are generally available.

I do not recommend particular motels or restaurants. The excellent cuisine of today may well vanish with tomorrow's new owner, as the restaurant degenerates into a greasy spoon. And old motels that once were clean and reasonably priced, if a little threadbare, may turn into dirty fleabags.

You can make reservations in advance, in a number of ways, particularly if the trip is to be a four- or five-day hike. Travel agencies have information on

Rogue River in the Wild Rogue Wilderness

Blacklock Point

the better-quality motels. Excellent resources for members are the American Automobile Association publications. The facilities described are AAA subscribers; other non-subscriber facilities do exist.

Most towns have chambers of commerce. A letter or phone call directed to these organizations should bring a flood of material.

Another method of finding a room is to call directory assistance and ask the operator to give the phone numbers of some motels in the town where you wish to stay. This method presumes a willing, friendly telephone operator. The first motel I called had rates that were higher than I was willing to pay. The second proved to be old, clean, and very reasonably priced.

Party Size

In the event of injury it is always desirable to leave a person with the victim while someone else goes for help. On most of these hikes, a minimum of three people will do. However, in the remote sections, such as Cape Blanco, two people should go for help to look after each other, so a party of four is best. Don't stay home because there are only two, but keep safety in mind when choosing a day's hike. Remember, an injured solo hiker may wait for an eternity.

Distances and Hiking Time

It is very difficult to compute accurate distances on beaches, with all their ins and outs and ups and downs. Moreover, beach miles do not readily compare to trail miles because the two surfaces vary so greatly.

For example, estimates of hiking times are based on a rate of 2½ miles per hour on hard sand. If the tide covers the hard sand, a hiker driven up onto soft sand, cobblestones, or driftwood may slow down to one mile per hour or less.

The small sketch maps at the beginning of each section are only intended to give a hiker a general location and point out a few of the important landmarks. For accuracy, we have included the names of one or more available maps.

The USGS topographical maps are the most accurate, with a scale large enough to identify even small landmarks. They can be purchased at mountain equipment shops, sporting goods stores, or map stores, or by writing the U.S. Geological Survey, Federal Center, Denver, CO 80225. Unfortunately, many of these maps have not been revised in 20 years, so access trails and roads are badly outdated.

The alternatives are county road maps published by the Oregon Department of Transportation, State Highway Building, Salem, Oregon 97310. Ask for the key map and order only the maps pertaining to the ocean. These maps may be available in stores along the coast.

The U.S. Forest Service has an excellent map of the Oregon Dunes National Recreation Area and another showing both the Kalmiopsis and Wild Rogue wildernesses. Both maps are available at Forest Service offices.

Southern Oregon Coast Warning

In much of its southern section, the Oregon beach is remote from U.S. 101. In addition, great care must be taken from December through February, when high tides run completely up to the abutting cliffs. Swiftly advancing water can cause driftwood logs to trap the unwary. Plan your trip with tide table in hand so you are not trapped by the high tide.

Any time of year, listen to the weather reports to make sure you are not going onto a beach during a major storm, when high tides reach higher than expected.

START OR FINISH OF HIKE	— —1600 — — —	CONTOURS IN FEET
GUARD STATION		ROAD
POINT OF INTREST	•••••••••••• •••••••••••••••	OVERLAND TRAILS
TOWN	——·· ——	RIVER
CITY	—— — ——	STATE BORDER
CAMPING		

Osprey nest near Tenmile Creek

Poison oak, a common plant near the ocean

Young brown pelicans summer on Oregon's estuaries

Logging ship on the Columbia River at Astoria

Salmon River and Salmon River headland

Holes in sandstone drilled by piddock clams

Rogue River in the Wild Rogue Wilderness

Heceta Head Lighthouse

Above: *Kelp*. Left: *Willet*.
Below: *Cannon Beach*

Above: *Tide pool with sea anemones and starfish.* Left: *Sand pendulum.* Below: *Common murres on Right Island from Yaquina Head Lighthouse*

Bald eagle near Harts Cove

Cannon Beach at low tide

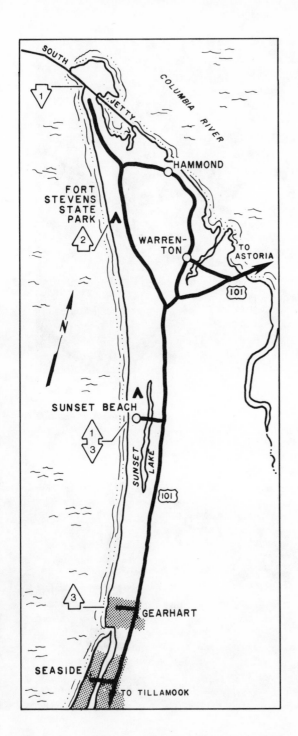

SOUTH

JETTY

COLUMBIA RIVER

1

HAMMOND

FORT
STEVENS
STATE
PARK

2

WARREN-
TON

TO
ASTORIA

101

N

SUNSET BEACH

1
3

SUNSET LAKE

101

3

GEARHART

SEASIDE

TO TILLAMOOK

SECTION A.
Columbia River to Seaside

Hikes along this section of the Oregon coast start at the mouth of the Columbia River and run 18 miles down the coast to the colorful town of Seaside. History buffs and marine enthusiasts can get into the spirit of the journey by first exploring the historic seaport of Astoria.

Oregon history started at the mouth of the Columbia near Astoria. Settlement spread rapidly southward into Seaside, along level terrain, until the bulk of Tillamook Head formed an obstacle. Near Astoria you'll find an old city to explore, a maritime museum, the Astor Column, a coastal defense fort, and Fort Clatsop. There are two excellent, long hikes along flat beaches.

To better understand the history of the Oregon coast, plan to spend a half day in Astoria, an ancient settlement by Oregon territory standards. Originally a fur trapping post, it's an interesting, colorful town. A slender, breathtaking toll bridge spans the Columbia here—a good photographic subject.

The place to start in Astoria is at the Columbia River Maritime Museum and lightship *Columbia* moored at the Coast Guard dock next door. The museum is located next to the river on the east side of town. Be sure to look at the photographs of the sailing ship *Peter Iredale*, wrecked 75 years ago. Compare that with what remains of the ship (see Hike 1). The binnacle and other artifacts of the *Peter Iredale* are also on display.

The lightship *Columbia* was for years anchored off the mouth of the Columbia River. Her crew must have been terribly bored rocking in the waves for months on end with only a foghorn to break the monotony. The *Columbia* was built in 1909 and named for her famous predecessor, piloted by Captain Gray. During World War II she was fitted with gun decks and antiaircraft artillery. Various changes were made in her superstructure over the years. The *Columbia* has been retired and now serves as a marine research laboratory.

The next stop should be the Astor Column, a 125-foot tower on a 700-foot hill overlooking Astoria. Inside the column is a steep spiral staircase, leading to an observation deck, surrounded by a slender, insecure-looking railing. From the deck extend broad views of the Columbia River, the bridge leading to Washington State, the Pacific Ocean, and Saddle Mountain—a 3283-foot mountain in the Coast Range (see Hike 63). This is a fine spot to visualize the history of the area. Look westward where the Lewis and Clark Expedition built Fort Clatsop and spent the winter of 1805. On the river below, John Jacob Astor founded a trading post in 1811. Farther out is the ill-famed Co-

Lightship Columbia *at Columbia River Maritime Museum, Astoria*

lumbia River Bar where over 100 ships have perished.

After leaving the Astor Column, you might want to round out your historical tour of the area by taking the following side trip into neighboring Washington. Cross the Columbia River toll bridge on U.S. 101 and on the north side of the river follow the highway west to the town of Ilwaco. At the Ilwaco cemetary, read the worn letters chiseled into the marble gravestones of the many seamen who lost their lives on the Columbia River Bar.

While in the state of Washington, go to the State Park Museum at Fort Canby. The whole story of the Lewis and Clark journey is documented here in words, pictures, and exhibits. There is also a section devoted to the history of the Coast Guard. Of special interest is the complicated prism of an old kerosene-burning lighthouse.

Back at Astoria, watch the ocean-going freighters loading at the city dock. Finally, drive 5 miles west on U.S. 101 and follow directions to Fort Clatsop, which has been reconstructed by the National Park Service from Meriwether Lewis's sketches.

From Astoria, take a bus or drive westward to Warrenton. Then hike or drive 4 miles to Fort Stevens State Park Campgound (don't confuse this with Fort Stevens Historical Site). From the campground, it is 4 miles north to the south jetty of the Columbia River. (Other than this campground there are no established campgrounds, but adjacent towns have motels.)

The south jetty marks the beginning of the Oregon Coast Trail system, which will eventually extend from the Columbia River to California. At present, the first 62 miles of continuous trail and beach walking have been designated. The trail markers are unobtrusive but very distinctive 6- to 8-foot cedar posts. While car travelers may never notice the markers, hikers will have no difficulty identifying others after seeing one.

A few other short sections of the trail are finished, but they have not been tied in with the system. Considering the many obstacles along the way, it may be years before the trail is complete. Anyone who hikes beyond the first 62 miles is a pioneer. Sometime in the future, when the trail is finished and thousands hike it, the way may seem easier, but those who pioneered the route will be glad they hiked it back in the good old days before it became crowded.

Oregon Coast Trail marker on a gray cedar post

1. SOUTH JETTY OF THE COLUMBIA RIVER TO SUNSET BEACH

Distance: 9 miles one way
Hiking time: 4 hours
Time of year: Any
Tide: Any
Obstacles: None
Map: Clatsop County #1
      (Oregon Dept. of Transportation)

The south jetty of the Columbia (4 miles north of Fort Stevens State Park Campground) is the beginning of the 358 miles of the Oregon coast. From the jetty one can look in almost a straight line down 15 miles of wide, sandy beaches to the town of Gearhart. The whole distance can be completed in one day, but you may have to contend with two shoes full of painful blisters; it is far better to take two days (see Hike 3).

Although the distance is right for a stopping point, there is no city near Sunset Beach. The traveler must either have a car waiting to drive to a motel, make a dry camp behind a sand dune, or plan to camp at Sunset Lake.

At the south jetty is an excellent wooden tower to climb. From 100 feet up you can see the extension of the jetty and a parade of ships: slow-moving freighters, deeply laden tankers, tug boats, pleasure boats. To the south runs the half-mile-wide margin of the beach, terminating at Tillamook Head with Seaside nestled in its crook.

Columbia River and Cape Disappointment Lighthouse in Washington from South Jetty

When you descend to the beach, civilization disappears. Smooth, easy sand encourages rapid progress. To the left are rolling sand dunes partially stabilized by coarse grass. The beach hiker, like the jogger, may be tempted to run. But the beachcomber will move slowly along exploring all those interesting nubbins — bird tracks, small mammal tracks, pieces of flotsam and jetsam cast up by the sea. Overhead wheel the crying glaucous gulls. Before you, the ballet dancers of the feathered world perform — the sandpipers pirouette and dip in graceful, coordinated movement. So it's raining. You've got the beach to yourself.

The dark hump of a shipwreck slowly grows, as does the number of people, until at 4 miles, you reach the *Peter Iredale*. There are restrooms near the wreck.

Here also is access to the Coffenbury Lake Campground, ¾ mile inland in Fort Stevens State Park (see Hike 2 for park trails). Backpackers can cook dinner here, where water is available, and then hike on another 4 or 5 miles before stopping for the night.

Sunset Beach access road appears at 10 miles. This road is the source of many of the cars that drive on the beach. Inland ½ mile is a private campground. The map shows it on Sunset Lake but it is signed Neacoxie Lake Campground. It seems to cater to RVs but advertises that it is also for tent campers. For driving instructions see Hike 3. The closest motels are south toward Gearhart.

2. FORT STEVENS STATE PARK

Distance: 2 to 7 miles round trip
Hiking time: 1 to 3 hours
Time of year: Any
Tide: Any
Obstacles: None
Map: State park brochure

Ten miles of hiking trails to walk, a shipwreck to photograph, and Battery Russell to explore — Fort Stevens is a good place to spend a day hiking or bicycling.

Fort Stevens State Park is 10 miles west of Astoria and 15 miles north of Seaside. The roads are well marked. In the parking areas, trailheads are also well marked. However, finding a sign telling where the trails go is not so easy, so pick up a map from a park ranger. You can, if you wish, drive to the points of interest in the park. But if you do, you will miss the miles of peaceful trails edged by 8-foot-high brush and, in the spring, you will not hear the cheerful song of the white-crowned sparrow, which is common on the Oregon coast.

The Peter Iredale *in 1906 (photo from the archives of the Columbia River Maritime Museum)*

The Peter Iredale *in 1949 – the bowsprit still intact*

The Peter Iredale *in 1983, showing its gradual disintegration*

At the campground-reception area find both the hiking and bicycle trail in the northwest corner near the bulletin board; hike 1 mile to the beach. The first stop is the wreck of the *Peter Iredale*. If the tide is in and the wreck surrounded by water, go first to Battery Russell and return a few hours later when the tide is out far enough to walk around the ship's remains.

The *Peter Iredale*, a four-masted British bark, came ashore on October 24, 1906. The ship's crew was rescued by the lifesaving crew at Point Adams, near the town of Hammond, and everything that could be removed was salvaged. Some of the artifacts and some large photographs taken shortly after the ship ran aground are on display at the Columbia River Maritime Museum in Astoria (see Section A introduction). These photographs show the bowsprit, which was still attached in the 1950s, but even that disappeared in 1963. Bit by bit the ship has rusted away and been covered by sand. All that is left now is a skeleton.

Next, hike to Battery Russell, built in 1863 to defend the Columbia River from a possible Confederate invasion that never occurred. The battery was manned again during World War I and again nothing happened. However, during World War II, on June 21, 1942, a Japanese submarine fired some random shots. The battery became the only coastal defense on the West Coast that was ever fired upon. The shots were fired from such a great distance and were so ineffective that Battery Russell didn't think it worthwhile to return the fire.

To reach the battery from the shipwreck, hike back toward the campground for ¾ mile. Opposite Coffenbury Lake take the mile-long trail heading north.

There are several possible return trails.

In addition to these trails, the park offers a ½-mile self-guided nature trail and a 2½-mile trail around Coffenbury Lake.

In the state park are car-camping facilities and, for anyone arriving on foot, a hiker-biker camp which has lower rates.

---

3. SUNSET BEACH TO GEARHART

Distance: 6 miles one way
Hiking time: 3 hours
Time of year: Any
Tide: Any
Obstacles: None
Map: Clatsop County #1 and #2
      (Oregon Dept. of Transportation)

A few years ago, romantic glass balls originally used as floats for Japanese fishing nets would occasionally appear on the beach. Crossing the ocean on

Mouth of the Necanicum River from Gearhart

the Japanese current, they were cast up onto the beach, frequently into the driftwood, by the passing storms, and usually partially buried. The hiker hastened by, but the beachcomber would poke among the driftwood, and just maybe.... These days, you probably won't find a glass ball, but you might uncover an oddly shaped piece of driftwood or a rock with an attractive color or a strange hole ground into it by a barnacle. You are sure to find plenty of bleach bottles and old tennis shoes.

Much of the distance from the south jetty of the Columbia River to Gearhart is far from buildings and roads and protected from civilization by a ½-mile-wide mixture of swamps and sand dunes. However, the area will not qualify for wilderness because cars are free to speed along the beach.

To reach Sunset Beach, drive 5 miles north from Gearhart on U.S. 101 and turn left at a sign pointing to Sunset Beach. Pass a golf course, Sunset Lake, and a commercial campground. In 1 mile you reach the ocean. There is limited parking near the beach.

Walk south on the smooth, wide beach toward Tillamook Head, the landmark at the far end of the beach. One of the surprising things about this beach is the lack of wood. While elsewhere beaches are lined with driftwood, there is virtually none here. Because of its dams, the Columbia River no longer carries much wood to the sea; thanks to the intervening sand dunes, there are no trees to topple off onto the beach. The beach may lack driftwood, but it is a haven for shore birds. Along the edge of the water in summer and winter are regiments of little sandpipers feeding, running in step, and flying in unison like an army drill team.

At 5 miles below a deluxe motel condominium, pass a beach access leading into Gearhart. At 6 miles, the beach ends at the mouth of the Necanicum River. Gearhart is a quiet town with several stores and motels but no campgrounds.

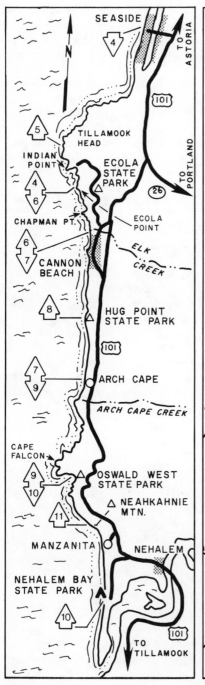

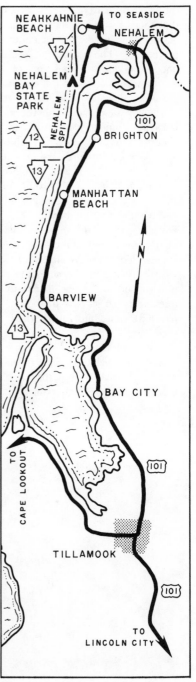

SECTION B.
Seaside to Tillamook

What to do in Seaside? You can take a dip in the public swimming pool or visit a commercial aquarium featuring seals. On the city's oceanfront you can walk, bicycle, skateboard, or jog along a mile-long walkway, with hotels on one side and the ocean on the other. Or you can visit the Lewis and Clark Expedition's salt cairn where, in 1806, the expedition's crew boiled saltwater continuously, 24 hours a day, for several months to produce 20 gallons of salt for preserving meat. (The salt cairn was reconstructed from one of Meriwether Lewis's sketches.) At the Historical Museum you'll find displays on North Coast Indians and logging, and a wall of vintage photographs.

When you tire of these activities, you can dress in as few clothes as is legal and join the multitudes stretched out on the beach. You might also hike the 1½ miles of beach in front of Seaside, viewing the panorama of architectural designs in homes and motels of this long-time resort community.

Twelfth Avenue bridge and Necanicum River

A few miles south of Seaside, U.S. 101 veers right at a junction with Highway 26, which continues straight ahead (southeastward) toward Portland. U.S. 101 continues south, winding up and over a small crest, then dropping down to a well-marked junction with a road that forks right into the town of Cannon Beach. That road rejoins the highway in a few miles.

U.S. 101 now drops down to ocean level and runs along past homes and tiny settlements to the massive bulk of Neahkahnie Mountain and Cape Falcon, which presented a major obstacle for the Indians and early settlers. The highway passes through a tunnel and winds upward, past Short Sands State Park, to a magnificent overlook at Neahkahnie Point. Southward lies magnificent Nehalem Point.

The highway now winds downward and leaves the ocean to go around Nehalem Bay, rejoining the water at Brighton. U.S. 101 runs with the ocean to Barview, where it turns inward behind Tillamook Bay to the town of Tillamook.

There is an excellent trail system that extends from the town of Seaside up over Tillamook Head to near Cannon Beach. From Cannon Beach to Arch Cape is excellent beach hiking. From Arch Cape over Neahkahnie Mountain and Cape Falcon extends a well-developed trail system with a very fine tent campground. From Neahkahnie to the end of the Nehalem Spit and back to the campground the travel is over compact sand. Beyond the spit from Brighton to Barview is good beach hiking, with mostly smooth sand. The section from Barview south to Tillamook is best traveled by highway.

---

4. SEASIDE TO ECOLA POINT

Distance: 11 miles one way
Hiking time: 6 hours
Time of year: Any
Tide: Any
Obstacles: Headland to cross
Map: Clatsop County #2
      (Oregon Dept. of Transportation)

The climb over 1200-foot-high Tillamook Head is one of the highlights of the Oregon coast. Besides being part of the Oregon Coast Trail, it has also been designated a National Scenic Trail. This can be a hard day's hike due to the elevation gain but provides excellent views. It can be shortened by terminating the hike at Indian Point.

From Seaside, hike the beach southward for an easy mile. When the beach bends westward and sand gives way to cobblestones, walk another ½ mile and locate a scramble trail climbing 250 feet to a road. The presence of ever-

Tillamook Head from Seaside

steepening cliffs means the traveler has missed the scramble trail. Return. Don't attempt to climb the rocks.

Follow the road past a golf course to its head, where there are a few parking places. (For a shorter hike you can drive to this point.) A substantial trail sign marks the entry into Elmer Feldenheimer Forest Reserve. To the left (west) is a small scramble trail that leads to a breathtaking view of the surf below, at the foot of a dangerous and unfenced cliff. Use caution at the cliff edge, especially if children are along.

The Elmer Feldenheimer trail switchbacks up through forests which, in mid-June, have a covering of colorful miner's lettuce. At an unmarked boundary, the trail leaves the forest reserve and enters Ecola State Park. In a short 2 miles, the traveler reaches an 1100-foot-high viewpoint. The view over Tillamook Head reaches to the north past Seaside and the sweep of the beach up toward the Columbia.

Where there was once an overnight camp there is now only a portable toilet approached by a forest road. The trail passes through a small clearcut created when windfalls were removed from the park following a storm. Following switchbacks down a descending slope, the trail reaches an overlook to the west. Here, under the magnificent arms of a very large tree, is a view of Tillamook Lighthouse (see the next section for a history and description).

The trail now descends through the forest, then outward to a view of Indian Point. The trail enters the Indian Point parking lot at the restrooms. The traveler can terminate the hike here or cross the parking lot and travel another mile of trail to Ecola Point. Cannon Beach offers the nearest overnight facilities.

5. TILLAMOOK HEAD

Distance: 4 to 6 miles round trip
Hiking time: 2 to 3 hours
Time of year: Any
Tide: Any
Obstacles: Headland to climb
Map: Clatsop County #2
      (Oregon Dept. of Transportation)

This is a hike to take advantage of the view–up and down the coast, far out toward China, and, closer at hand, to a picturesque lighthouse on a tiny island offshore. This is a round-trip hike, taking in a portion of Hike 4.

Beach at Indian Point from Oregon Coast Trail

Oregon Coast Trail over Tillamook Head

At the north end of the town of Cannon Beach, turn west on a road signed "Ecola State Park." The road is paved but extremely winding and narrow. In 2 miles it reaches Ecola Point, a popular picnic area. It is well worth walking the paved trail out to the edge of the point for the great view looking south toward Cannon Beach and Haystack Rock. Turning left at the tollbooth at the entry of Ecola Point, the traveler can drive another 1½ miles to the end of the road at Indian Point.

The trail starts on the north side of the Indian Point parking lot. In 100 feet or so, the trail forks; go left. The trail climbs through a forest with a ground cover of salal and salmonberry, and gaps in the trees allow great views. In ½ mile, after gaining 300 feet of elevation, you reach Indian Point.

Standing under a knarred tree, you can see Tillamook Lighthouse, built around 1880 on a small offshore island. The problem of building on the island was horrendous, and there was at least one fatality. During fierce winter storms, giant waves inundated the entire lighthouse. Because the lighthouse could only be reached in the best weather, it was eventually abandoned and is now slowly being reclaimed by the sea. It's accessible only by helicopter under most circumstances. For more on this amazing lighthouse, read James Gibbs' book, *Tillamook Light*. Legend has it that the rock was purchased, sight unseen, by some gambling interests out of Nevada. We haven't tried to verify this ownership, since to do so might destroy an interesting legend.

Telephoto of Tillamook Lighthouse

Two miles farther, at approximately 900 feet elevation, you reach Tilla-mook Head. Don't stop here. Instead, continue northward through another 2 miles of forest to enjoy a view to the north before turning back. For a change of scenery on the return trip, walk by the portable toilet down the seldom, if ever, used radar road, which winds its way into the moist valley of Indian Creek and back to the starting point.

For a variety of ocean views, hike the Oregon Coast Trail from Indian Beach 1½ miles to Ecola Point. If transportation can be arranged, do it just one way. However, anyone hiking it both ways will get double enjoyment.

---

6. ECOLA POINT TO CANNON BEACH

Distance: 2 miles round trip
              2½ miles one way
Hiking time: 1 hour round trip
                2 hours one way
Time of year: Any
Tide: Any
Obstacles: None
Map: Clatsop County #2
       (Oregon Dept. of Transportation)

This is really two hikes, a short round trip on the beach to the jagged tooth of Chapman Point, and a one-way hike from Ecola Point to the quaint town of

Deer at Ecola State Park

Cannon Beach. Both of these hikes take you along a wide stretch of sand fringed with gnarled, silvery driftwood.

To reach the Ecola Point parking lot, where these hikes begin, see Hike 5.

ROUND TRIP TO CHAPMAN POINT. From the Ecola Point parking lot, a paved trail leads downward toward the point and onto Crescent Beach. This is a big, sandy beach, a delight to hike on, but it ends in a short mile at Chapman Point. Above the beach is a steep hillside covered with slide alder, ultimately leveling out to a small hilltop of fir and deciduous trees. (The trail referred to below wanders along this hilltop.)

The hike terminates at an obviously impassable point. Do not use the scramble trail that appears just before the point, since it ends on private property and the owners have obviously been much annoyed by trespassing. However, the trip back is as delightful as the trip going.

ONE WAY TO CANNON BEACH. Walk southward on the road out of the Ecola Point parking lot. In a short ⅛ mile, a trail entrance leads downward and along the bluff for approximately one mile. Just before leaving the bluff, you'll have a view of the beach below.

Where the trail ends, at a road, parking is obviously discouraged by a series of rocks, posts, rails, etc. There has been a trespass problem with people coming off the end of Chapman Beach, up a scramble trail and into someone's backyard. The park department, rather than creating a trail for legal exit, has elected to put in the posts and rocks to discourage parking. This seems an exercise in futility.

Walk the road a scant ¼ mile to 7th Street in Cannon Beach, where a sign says, "No Beach Access." This sign is for automobiles. People on foot can follow 7th Street downhill, turn left on an unimproved street, and turn right on 6th Street to reach Chapman Beach.

On the beach, head south for ½ mile until Elk Creek blocks the way. Turn inland to the state park road, cross Elk Creek on a bridge and enter the town of Cannon Beach, where there are a private campground, a hostel, and a number of motels.

An unmarked bus stop is located on the main street between 1st Street and 2nd Street, in front of Sandpiper Square.

7. CANNON BEACH TO ARCH CAPE

Distance: 7 miles one way
Hiking time: 2 to 3 hours
Time of year: Any
Tide: Low to medium
Obstacles: 3 points to round
Map: Clatsop County #2
      (Oregon Dept. of Transportation)

At low tide the whole distance can be hiked on a sandy beach past numerous rocky islands and under steep rock cliffs with interesting caves and waterfalls.

Before starting the hike, take a quick look around the town of Cannon Beach. It won't take long, as there is only one main street. This is a resort town that looks like a resort town should, with tasteful old-fashioned stores of weathered gray. During the summer it will be awash with tourists browsing in interesting shops, including grocery stores.

The small cannon for which the town was named can be seen in a roadside park along U.S. 101. On September 10, 1846, the U.S.S. *Shark*, on a mission to make depth soundings in the Columbia River channel, wrecked on the Columbia River bar. The ship broke up and drifted southward, and a few days later part of the deck with the cannon attached washed ashore at the townsite. The wreckage was probably the bow, for not only was the cannon saved but also the capstan for pulling up the anchor, which is also on display.

The town's beach is great for strolling, especially at low tide when there are rocks and tidal pools to explore. To get to the beach – and the beginning of the hike – drive to the large city parking lot and walk just two city blocks.

Start the hike where Elk Creek empties into the ocean, at the north end of Cannon Beach. Walk south past hotels and houses. In one mile pass Haystack Rock. Notice the warning signs – people sunning themselves on the rock have frequently been stranded by an incoming tide. It is a long 6- to 8-hour wait for the tide to go out, and if the weather turns bad, sunbathers may have to be rescued, an embarrassing, expensive operation.

At 1¾ miles, pass a large public parking area with restrooms. Next are three small points. Unless the tide is way out, one may have to scramble up to the highway to get around Silver, Humbug, and Hug points. At Hug Point, see the old roadway bed blasted in the side of the cliff. The history of this point is explained in Hike 8.

Tillamook Lighthouse from Cannon Beach

Silver, Humbug, and Hug Points with Cape Falcon in distance

The trip ends where Arch Cape Creek meets the ocean next to the vertical face of Arch Cape. Just follow the street upward to a public access near the U.S. 101 bridge.

There are two small stores at the community of Arch Cape, but the closest accommodations are back toward Cannon Beach. Backpackers might get water at Hug Point State Park and find a campsite on the beach out of sight of houses, or continue 7 more miles to the walk-in campsite at Shore Sand Beach (Hike 9).

8. HUG POINT

Distance: 1 mile round trip
Hiking time: ½ hour
Time of year: Any
Tide: Medium
Obstacles: None
Map: Clatsop County #2
        (Oregon Dept. of Transportation)

Hug Point doesn't offer much hiking, but you will find a fascinating bit of history to contemplate, some small caves to explore, and tall cliffs to admire.

From the resort city of Cannon Beach, drive south 4 miles on U.S. 101 to Hug Point State Park, a day-use area only a few steps from the beach.

Fall Creek and caves at Hug Point

Walk north to the first cliff. In April a colony of pigeon guillemots nest on the cliffs. These are black birds with white wing patches and bright red legs. They feed out on the ocean but come ashore to nest. The "nests" on the cliffs appear to be just sticks or grass lining niches in the rock. As soon as the chicks are old enough to fly off the cliff, they leave and never return to the nest.

The second cove north contains a waterfall and some interesting caves. The

Old road on side of Hug Point

waterfall, on Fall Creek, varies in size with the season. Beside it is a cave big enough to walk in, but judging from the amount of driftwood jammed in the upper end, it would not be a snug place to sit out a storm.

As you go north, the next cliff you encounter is Hug Point, where a narrow road was blasted in the rock. Since prehistoric times in North America, ocean beaches served as paths for Indian travelers. When white settlers arrived, they used the beaches as wagon roads. Now hikers are using the same beaches for recreation. Headlands have always been a problem, causing long waits for low tides. Headlands that couldn't be rounded at any time were crossed by overland wagon trails.

Hug Point was so named because wagons had to dash between waves, hugging the point to get around. Wagons eventually changed to automobiles. Many years ago, Ray Brown, who lives in nearby Neahkahnie Beach, was rounding the point in his Maxwell automobile when it became trapped in sand. Before the car could be rescued, the tide came in. After the water retreated, he salvaged the car, dried it out, and continued to drive it.

After this incident, a road was blasted in the cliff just wide enough for one Model T or Maxwell at a time. The road is just a bit above the low tide mark and covered by water the rest of the time. Hikers can walk this road and see for themselves how the rock was cut. There remains even a little bit of the cement used to fill in cracks in the rock.

The tiny community of Neahkahnie Beach, where Ray Brown lives, is visible below U.S. 101 just south of the highway tunnel through Arch Cape. All of the older homes were built of materials transported around Hug Point and Arch Cape at low tide. The settlement was created from the beach up – the steep road that leads down from U.S. 101 into Neahkahnie was built relatively recently.

---

9. ARCH CAPE TO SHORT SAND BEACH

Distance: 6 miles one way
Hiking time: 3 to 4 hours
Time of year: Any
Tide: Any
Obstacles: Headland to cross
Map: Clatsop County #2
      (Oregon Dept. of Transportation)

Hidden beaches, spectacular headlands, forest trails, the eerie cry of a cougar, and a sweeping view from the top of 1631-foot Neahkahnie Mountain are all within Oswald D. West State Park, named for the governor responsible for keeping Oregon's beaches public.

Oregon Coast Trail bridge over Arch Cape Creek

The hike through the park can be done in one long day, but there are a variety of trails that demand attention, so the park has been divided into three trips (hikes 9, 10, and 11).

At the south end of the community of Arch Cape, before the highway reaches a bridge and a tunnel, turn east on Arch Cape Mill Road. In ¼ mile the road turns left and becomes Webb Street. In another ¼ mile find a driveway on the right side marked only with a cedar post engraved with the Oregon Coast Trail insignia. Follow the driveway past a house to Arch Cape Creek.

The trail begins with a suspension bridge and then follows switchbacks up through heavy timber, gaining 400 feet in about one mile. Cedar posts mark where the Oregon Coast Trail crosses U.S. 101 (about ½ mile south of the tunnel at the first pull out) and continue another mile to an unmarked crossing over the Neahkahnie Beach Road.

An alternate route to this point is to round Arch Cape at low tide, hike past the community of Neahkahnie Beach, and go up the access road toward U.S. 101. The point where the trail leaves the access road is unmarked but obvious.

Do not attempt to continue around the point to the south of Nehalem Beach. The route is not only impassable, but very dangerous.

From the last crossing of the Neahkahnie Beach Road, it is 2¼ miles to Cape Falcon. The trail crosses Elk Flats (considering the number of elk tracks in the vicinity, the flats are probably well named), then climbs an unnamed hill, skirting the crest to reach a great view of Cape Falcon.

The cape is a rocky cliff without beaches, where you'll discover a variety of terrain, headlands with windswept meadows, salal, alders, and evergreens. Below are sea caves and vertical cliffs with surf crashing against their base. (It was here my wife and a lady friend, traveling a little more slowly, heard the screams of an unseen cougar, an impressive and a bit scary experience.) Take time out to walk a side trail onto the cape itself. Several little side trails lead to where you can look down on the boiling surf. Not too close, please!

The Oregon Coast Trail now curves inland to Short Sand Beach on Smugglers Cove, in Oswald West State Park, the end of the day's hike.

The beach is a delight, and in the woods is a walk-in campground ¼ mile from U.S. 101. In the campground are a modern restroom, over 30 campsites, and wheelbarrows to carry a tent and other gear from the parking lot. There is the usual charge for camping plus the special surcharge for out-of-state visitors. You can sleep here under the tall trees halfway between the noise of U.S. 101 and the sound of pounding surf. From the campground, several trails climb up to the highway. Each has charm, is worth exploring, and lends itself to a loop trip.

An alternate round trip would be to park at Short Sand parking lot and hike down to the beach. Here the traveler turns south and then westward on the trail to Cape Falcon. This is a trip short enough for children, but watch them carefully above the cliffs of the cape.

10. SHORT SAND BEACH TO NEHALEM BAY STATE PARK

Distance: 8 miles one way
Hiking time: 4 to 5 hours
Time of year: Any
Tide: Any
Obstacles: Mountain to cross
Map: Tillamook County #1
   (Oregon Dept. of Transportation)

The Oregon Coast Trail climbs over Neahkahnie Mountain, giving an eye-popping view of the ocean, then descends to a campground on a sandy spit between the ocean and a quiet bay. The way passes through several large meadows, the first of many on the Oregon coast. There are several theories about why the meadows exist. Some authorities believe they are the result of fires; others think they are the result of storms and grazing.

From Short Sand Beach in Oswald West State Park, take the south trail. After a short, steep climb, the Oregon Coast Trail parallels the beach a ways, then traverses through grass-covered meadows above Neahkahnie Punch Bowl, an amphitheater of surging surf inaccessible on foot. A short side trail leads to the edge of the Punch Bowl. The cliffs are closed for the obvious reason that they are about to slide into the Punch Bowl. By skirting around the bushes, however, it's possible to gain a safe look down into the bowl. After approximately one mile at an elevation of 450 feet, the trail crosses U.S. 101 for the long climb over Neahkahnie Mountain.

At the crossing, you can walk up the highway ¼ mile to a paved overlook for a preview of the panorama from the summit of Neahkahnie Mountain. Here, at the Neahkahnie Point parking lot, you can also take a short side trip to an impressive view of sea caves. Go directly west over the short stone wall down to a scramble trail, which leads straight down the top of the steep-sided ridge. Views southward toward Manzanita beckon to the unwary, but do not attempt the climb down – it's too dangerous. Continue on the trail approximately ¼ mile to a rocky overlook. Stop at this safe point. While it is possible to scramble farther, there is danger of falling.

Looking to the north, you can see two giant tilted slabs leaning toward the east, with the sea surging behind them. For good photographs of these sea

Short Sand Beach Campground

Short Sand Beach and mouth of Short Sand Creek

caves a telephoto lens would be desirable.

The climb of Neahkahnie Mountain is described in Hike 11. In wet or stormy weather, it is recommended that hikers walk the road around the mountain instead of climbing over it.

11. NEAHKAHNIE MOUNTAIN

Distance: 5 miles round trip
Hiking time: 4 hours
Time of year: March to November
Tide: Any
Obstacles: Mountain to climb
Map: Tillamook County #1
      (Oregon Dept. of Transportation)

Whether hiking the Oregon coast from the Columbia River to California or just hitting a few highlights, don't miss this portion of the Oregon Coast Trail. It climbs to the 1631-foot summit of Neahkahnie Mountain, offering views up and down the coast. Near the summit, the tread narrows and the trail is quite exposed, so watch your step and keep small children close at hand. The trail goes over the mountain and down the other side, so it can be hiked in either direction. Even though the north approach is a mile longer, it is described here because it provides better views along the way.

From the community of Arch Cape, go south on U.S. 101 through a tunnel into Oswald West State Park. One mile past the picnic area, as the highway climbs a shoulder of Neahkahnie Mountain, park at a wide, graveled shoulder (the last parking place before reaching the paved viewpoints). Across the highway is the trailhead with an 8-foot-high cedar post, the Oregon Coast Trail marker. Elevation here is 470 feet.

The trail starts in a large meadow, where it runs beside a line of telephone poles. It is said that this is the roadbed the pioneers built in 1913 and probably used as a foot and horse trail before that. The trail leaves the pioneer road and switchbacks up the meadow, which is covered with huge sword ferns and

Neahkahnie Beach from top of Neahkahnie Mountain

Cape Falcon from Neahkahnie Mountain trail

salal. Beyond are views of the Punch Bowl, Smugglers Cove, and Cape Falcon. Near the top of the meadow, the trail enters a forest with dense underbrush, then moves onto the north side of the mountain, where very little grows on the forest floor.

In a short 2 miles the trail traverses back around the west shoulder of the mountain to the south side, drops a bit, then climbs from forest to a steep, rocky meadow. The tread narrows as the trail leads around a near-vertical, exposed hillside to a saddle only 100 feet from the top. At the saddle, leave the trail and scramble up the rocky ridge to the 1631-foot summit. Views range south to Cape Meares, north to Tillamook Head, east over the Coast Range, and west toward China. The summit is a rock garden with wild onions, sedums, and, in May, the beautiful pink coast fawn lily.

The recommended way down is to return on the same trail. However, for variety, continue on the Oregon Coast Trail, descending to U.S. 101 in 1½ miles, then walk a short mile back up the highway to the starting point. While the views are sensational along this section of the highway, the road is narrow and the traffic nerve-racking.

12. NEAHKAHNIE BEACH AND THE NEHALEM SPIT

Distance: 5 miles one way
    8 miles round trip to Nehalem Bay State Park boat launch
Hiking time: 2 hours one way
    3½ hours round trip
Time of year: Any
Tide: Any
Obstacles: Must arrange to cross river
Map: Tillamook County #1
    (Oregon Dept. of Transportation)

This day's hike, starting at Neahkahnie Beach, leads down a long, smooth beach out onto a long spit. From the end of the spit a boat trip can be arranged to cross the entrance of Nehalem Bay. As an alternative, you can take a round trip – just continue up the west side of Nehalem Bay, past the site of several shipwrecks, to a boat launch.

BOAT RIDE ONE WAY. If you're going to take the boat ride across Nehalem Bay, you can make telephone arrangements by calling Jetty Fisheries, (503) 368-5748, to arrange a time and price. There is a pay phone at Nehalem Bay State Park. (Camping in this park is much more attractive to those with wheeled camping facilities than to tent campers.)

At Neahkahnie Beach you might turn northward to follow the beach ½ mile to Neahkahnie Point before retracing your steps. Neahkahnie Beach is an old resort community almost immediately adjacent to Manzanita, also an old, quiet town.

From Manzanita it's 3½ miles down around the end of the spit to the relatively new breakwaters installed and repaired by the Coast Guard in 1980 and 1981. A wave to the folks on the other side will signal them to come across the narrow entrance to the bay in a small boat to carry you across. A more athletic hiker may continue on down to Barview (see Hike 13).

BAYSIDE ROUND TRIP. If you're not taking a boat, proceed northward from the end of the spit along the west side of Nehalem Bay. In 3 miles you will reach the public boat ramp of Nehalem Bay State Park; turn around here. This route, protected from offshore winds, shows a marked contrast to the ocean side of the spit. Here flourish numerous birds, grasses, and tiny mammals.

This section of beach has seen at least three shipwrecks. In February 1913 the German square-rigger *Mimi* ran aground at the south entrance of Nehalem Bay. The ship remained upright, and all hands escaped without difficulty. In a salvage effort, 1300 tons of ballast were removed. Giant anchors were placed offshore, and with the help of an extreme high tide and a donkey engine the ship was pulled off the beach – into a nasty wind and high surf. Without ballast the ship rolled over, trapping the workers. Four were saved, thanks to the heroic effort of Coast Guard surfmen in a whale boat, but 17 men were lost.

In October of the same year, the British full-rigged ship *Glenesslin* was seen with all sails set, running close to shore on a clear day. The ship suddenly veered toward shore and hit the rocks below Neahkahnie Mountain. A rescue line was shot from the ship to the rocks. All 21 crewmen reached safety but the vessel was a total loss. A court of inquiry held the officers responsible for what was alleged to be the intoxicated condition of the crew. The master's certificate was removed for three months, the second mate's for six months, and the first mate was reprimanded.

It was an era in which steamships had made sailing ships obsolete. The sailing ships tended to be manned by the inexperienced, the inept, and the rejects of the merchant marine world.

The third loss, and the most interesting perhaps, is a legendary shipwreck involving a cargo of beeswax in the Manzanita area. Since a block of this beeswax can be found in the Tillamook museum, the espisode is described in the Section C introduction.

Neahkahnie Beach and Neahkahnie Mountain

Twin Rocks near town of Rockaway

13. NEHALEM BAY TO BARVIEW

Distance: 7 miles one way
Hiking time: 2 hours
Time of year: Any
Tide: Any
Obstacles: None
Map: Tillamook County #1
    (Oregon Dept. of Transportation)

Seven miles of uninterrupted sandy beach reward the hiker along this portion of the coast. The entrance of Nehalem Bay with its jetties is clearly visible from the highway. There is a small grocery store where the traveler's car can probably be parked. Please ask permission from the owners (purchase of goodies for the trip would be appropriate). They also specialize in bringing hikers across from the Manzanita Spit.

Walk down the south jetty past the tiny Coast Guard station until you reach the beach and a seven-mile hike over firm, pleasant sands. During the first mile there are a few homes and rolling sand dunes to the left. The town of Manhattan Beach merges into Rockaway; both of these communities have motels. Eventually, after 6 miles, the beach swings away from U.S. 101. The next stretch extends over a mile without cabins, eventually reaching the north jetty on Tillamook Bay.

At the jetty, take the asphalt road into Barview and to U.S. 101. Just before Barview is a county park, which has one section with hookups for trailers and motor homes. A second section is particularly pleasant for tent campers. Picnic tables are scattered about in small openings in the trees where there is some privacy and wind protection. It's one of the nicest tent-camping places along the Oregon coast.

Barview consists of only a gas station, a general store, and a few homes. Theoretically it would be possible to hire a fisherman to take the traveler southward across to Bay Ocean Peninsula, but it's a remote possibility because of the quietness of the community. It's now 12 miles by road into Tillamook past Bay City, a hustling and bustling fishing community with a marina, stores, and restaurants.

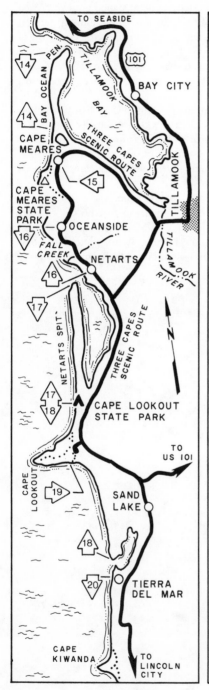

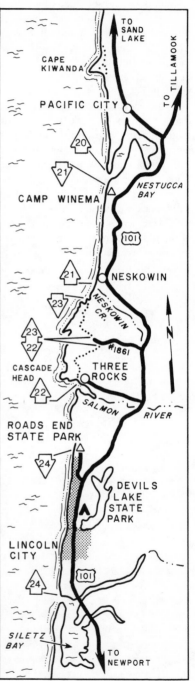

SECTION C.

Tillamook to Lincoln City

This section of coast extends from the pastoral Tillamook region south to the energetic tourist center of Lincoln City. Highway 101 turns inland at the town of Tillamook and does not return to the coast until 27 miles later, at Oretown. This drive through the lovely Tillamook Valley, with its picture-book dairy farms, is worthwhile in its own right. But eager coast hikers will want to take the following route.

At Tillamook turn west off U.S. 101, following signs to Cape Meares and the Three Capes Scenic Route. After two miles, just beyond the bridge over the Tillamook River, turn right. This route is, indeed, scenic – narrow, winding, with many ups and downs. It passes Cape Meares (an interesting side stop), the tiny community of Oceanside (a short ⅛ mile to the right), and the community of Netarts. At the next junction turn right, following the road to the town of Sand Lake. Again turn right. Drive past Cape Kiwanda to Pacific City and onto the junction with U.S. 101. Southward, the highway turns right, climbs abruptly up and over a high shoulder, and eventually comes into Lincoln City.

The hiking terrain starts at the long spit of Bay Ocean Peninsula and extends up over Cape Meares to the lighthouse. From here it's by road to Oceanside. There is a nice beach walk from Oceanside to Netarts. Beyond is another inlet with Netarts Spit just across the way. Then trails run up past Cape Lookout, back down to the beach, and southward on the beach to Sand Lake. Beyond the entrance to Sand Lake is excellent beach hiking to Pacific City, with its spit to the south. South of the spit is a short section of good beach terminating at Neskowin. Beyond, Cascade Head offers a magnificent overlook and a Nature Conservancy trail. Finally, there is a long section of excellent beach at Lincoln City.

The town and valley of Tillamook are picturesque and well worth exploration. Agriculture came early to this area, culminating in the Tillamook cheddar cheeses, which are largely produced by the Tillamook Cooperative. The cooperative's cheese factory, a handsome gathering of buildings with a repro-duction of an early local sailing vessel mounted in front, is located just north of town. Tours are conducted through the cooperative plant, and cheese samples are provided. In addition, the cooperative sells other excellent dairy products, including delicious ice cream cones.

Do not miss the Pioneer Museum in downtown Tillamook. There is a small

Bay Ocean Peninsula and Cape Meares

charge for entry; it's well worth planning to spend several hours here. It exhibits an excellent collection of pioneer materials, clothing, home utensils, furniture, and even farm equipment and carriages (in the basement). In addition, the museum is a memorial center for World War I and World War II dead, with interesting pictures and antique military equipment.

Of special interest is a large block of wax with strange inscriptions that was recovered from the area near Neahkahnie and Manzanita Spit. The block was apparently left behind from a shipwreck. Historians speculate that the ship was Spanish, en route to the Orient with a cargo of beeswax (a regular commodity), but driven northward by a storm. An old Indian legend tells of shipwrecked sailors burying a cargo of beeswax, then killing a black man and burying him on top of the cargo as a warning to the Indians. Unfortunately, the legend cannot be verified.

14. BAY OCEAN PENINSULA (TILLAMOOK SPIT) TO CAPE MEARES

Distance: 7 miles one way
Hiking time: 3½ hours one way
Time of year: Any
Tide: Any
Obstacles: None
Map: Tillamook County #1
   (Oregon Dept. of Transportation)

On this hike along sandy beaches, you can read the story of a city consumed by the Pacific Ocean.

From the city center of Tillamook, drive westward past the new hospital for 2 miles and turn right at the Cape Meares junction. Drive about a mile to another junction – this one with a road that heads off to the right across a

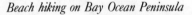

Beach hiking on Bay Ocean Peninsula

causeway leading onto the Bay Ocean Peninsula. For a brief history of the Bay Ocean Park development, read the sign immediately to the left (west) of the causeway. Turn right at the junction and cross the causeway on the lower (eastern) road and stop in the parking lot. The lake to the left of the causeway is the site of the ill-fated Bay Ocean Park.

In 1910, T. B. Potter envisioned for the peninsula a summer resort that would rival Atlantic City. After platting the development, substantial improvements were made, including creation of a natatorium with a 136-foot swimming pool, the Bay Ocean Hotel, and a dance hall. Approximately 20 homes were built, and streets with curbs were installed. Initial access was by boat, with a railroad anticipated for the future. By 1914, however, Bay Ocean Park Enterprises was bankrupt, and in the 1920s Bay Ocean Park was in full depression. Little by little the resort declined.

Installation of a single north jetty altered existing current patterns, causing the sea to eat away at the base of the spit. By 1932 the sea had nibbled away the natatorium, and by 1949 it had destroyed the last of the 20 homes. By 1952, the advancing sea had changed the spit into an island, as it appears on

the USGS map Nehalem. In 1956, the current breakwater and causeway were built to provide access to the south jetty, at the entrance of Tillamook Harbor. This new construction caused the once-destroyed beach to reform, thereby reconnecting the island with the mainland. The lake, formed by the reconstituted spit, and its adjacent swamp make a magnificent wild area and bird sanctuary.

Starting from the parking lot by the causeway, walk a gated road 3½ miles along Tillamook Bay on the east side of the peninsula and explore the 80-foot-high hills that were islands during the 1950s. There are fine campsites along this route but no water. Rounding the tip of the peninsula, hike the excellent ocean beach southward 5 miles to the tiny community of Cape Meares (no accommodations and limited parking).

You can walk the road back to your car or hike back up the beach, crossing to the north of the newly formed lake.

An alternative hike would be to start from the parking lot by the causeway and travel westward to the ocean beach over an established trail. Then, by turning northward, the traveler can do the trip around the peninsula in reverse.

Cape Meares Lighthouse

15. CAPE MEARES

Distance: 3 miles
Hiking time: 1 ½ hours
Time of year: Any
Tide: Medium to low
Obstacles: 500-foot elevation gain
Map: Tillamook County #1
    (Oregon Dept. of Transportation)

This hike features a 500-foot climb to the Cape Meares headland, plus a visit to Octopus Tree. A car can be left at each end for a shuttle.

From the parking area of the community of Cape Meares, walk the boulder-strewn beach south ½ mile at medium to low tide until the beach ends against the steep hillside of Cape Meares. Find the Oregon Coast Trail marker. The trail starts directly behind the sign, climbing through a small cleft onto a

The Octopus Tree

Fall Creek near Netarts

forested hillside. The trail, in excellent condition, was once a pioneer route. It probably was used by Indians long before the first white settlers arrived.

The way follows switchbacks, climbing steeply through timber and brush to a fork. The left fork goes to the highway. The right fork leads to Cape Meares and its parking area.

The Cape Meares lighthouse sits just below the level of the trail, which brings one face to face with the giant, complex prisms. During the summer season the building is open for an even closer examination. The lighthouse, now just an historic landmark, has been replaced by the automatic light just a few feet away.

Offshore islands hosting thousands of nesting birds are part of the national wildlife refuge system. On the north side of the cape two of the islands are so close that you can see that they are covered with birds. To really appreciate the sight, carry a pair of binoculars and a telephoto lens.

From the lighthouse walk back to the parking lot and past the restrooms to the Octopus Tree, a massive, misshapen spruce. The trail continues another ½ mile to the highway. You can turn back there or at the Cape Meares parking lot.

16. OCEANSIDE TO NETARTS

Distance: 2½ miles one way
Hiking time: 1¼ hours
Time of year: Any
Tide: Medium to low
Obstacles: In rainy season, a possibly difficult creek crossing
Map: Tillamook County #1
        (Oregon Dept. of Transportation)

Oceanside, located 2¾ miles south of Cape Meares, is a small community clinging to a mountainside. It is quite attractive, with motels ranging from moderate to expensive in price, as well as grocery stores and gas stations. Turn right at the town stop sign and follow the road through town to a public beach access. Hike south from here. This is an area of old cabins, spaced well apart. The road traverses just behind them, and beyond rise steep, heavily forested hills.

The beach provides excellent going, but during rainy periods you may have to wade Fall Creek, which is located just before Happy Camp. Note the stream-crossing warning in the "What You'll Need to Know" section in the front of this book. At 2½ miles from Oceanside you reach a public boat launch and a small marina at Netarts. A busy place on weekends, Netarts is an attractive community with restaurants, motels, and stores. There is an old trailer-tent camp at Happy Camp.

Clam digging at Netarts

Netarts boat launching ramp

17. NETARTS SPIT

Distance: 10 miles round trip
Hiking time: 5 hours
Time of year: Any
Tide: Any
Obstacles: None
Map: Tillamook County #2
    (Oregon Dept. of Transportation)

For much of its 5 miles, Netarts Spit is only a few hundred feet wide, encompassing a shallow bay barely a mile across. Opposite the town of Netarts, the bay narrows to a width of only 1000 feet.

The hike begins at Cape Lookout State Park, 5½ miles south of Netarts. At the Cape Lookout parking lot, find a big wooden sign with an engraved map showing the park trails. Take the one that heads north to Netarts Spit. You can walk north on one side of the spit and return south on the other.

Netarts Bay typifies coastal wetlands, which are often viewed only as potential building sites rather than the important marine nurseries and wildlife habitats that they actually are. In such marshes as this, flourishing plankton ensure the well-being of fish and other creatures along the food chain. Waterfowl, herons, and other birds are drawn to such bays because of the rich food supply.

The adventurous hiker can arrange a car shuttle by leaving one vehicle at Cape Lookout and driving back to the County Park boat launch at Netarts. With a big smile and a few dollars to pay for gas, you might persuade a fisherman to ferry you across the entrance of Netarts Bay to the spit. Or if that doesn't work, try the marina across the street, where boats are rented. One caution: the nearest bit of land is not the actual end of the spit, but a small island from which you can wade across to the spit proper only at low tide!

18. CAPE LOOKOUT STATE PARK TO SAND LAKE

Distance: 8½ miles one way
Hiking time: 5 hours
Time of year: Any
Tide: Any
Obstacles: Headland to cross, 800-foot elevation gain
Map: Tillamook County #2
(Oregon Dept. of Transportation)

On this hike a segment of the Oregon Coast Trail gains 800 feet on a forested path over Cape Lookout. It then descends to a wide, sandy beach, which runs 4½ miles to the outflow of Sand Lake.

The hike begins near the day-use parking lot at Cape Lookout State Park. To reach it, take the Three Capes Scenic Route, which runs along the shoreline west of U.S. 101. Cape Lookout State Park is 5½ miles south of the community of Netarts. At the Cape Lookout parking lot, find a big wooden sign with an engraved map showing the park trails. The Cape Lookout Trail starts nearby.

At the beginning, the trail is mostly level through woods. After ¼ mile the trail starts upward in a series of switchbacks, then makes a big bend into the Cape Creek drainage. After 2½ miles, at the top of an 800-foot-high saddle, is the edge of Cape Lookout. At this point are a large parking area and a large wooden signboard giving trail directions, including information on the Cape Lookout Trail (another worthwhile 4-mile detour – see Hike 19).

Fishing at the mouth of Sand River

No trail signs mark the trail down to the southern beach. Follow the Cape Lookout Trail a few hundred feet and find the beach trail—turn left and downward. The trail descends, then traverses the hillside in a series of final switchbacks to the beach, ¼ mile south of the near-vertical south face of Cape Lookout. You might consider walking northward to the end of the beach.

Continue southward down the beach on excellent sand, passing Camp Clark and, in another mile, Camp Meriwether, both Scout camps. In 4 miles you reach Sand Lake's narrow passageway to the sea, fed by Sand Creek and Jewel Creek.

The sand dunes in the vicinity of Sand Lake are partly on federal land and, thus, subject to multiple use. In this case, the dunes are single use—an ORV (off-road vehicles) playground with accompanying sound.

Near Sand Lake is a desirable campground. Unfortunately, the guests tune up their noisy machines and radios at odd times. You reach this campground by driving the Three Capes Scenic Route from Netarts south past Cape Lookout to the tiny community of Sand Lake. At the small store, turn right and drive 1.7 miles to the Forest Service campground. The campground is convenient, but heavy use by ORV campers will deter those seeking a quiet setting. Motels are available in Pacific City.

19. CAPE LOOKOUT

Distance: 4 miles round trip
Hiking time: 2 hours
Time of year: Any
Tide: Any
Obstacles: None
Map: Tillamook County #2
　　　(Oregon Dept. of Transportation)

This is an easy 2-mile trail out to the tip of Cape Lookout. The way is a pleasant mixture of forest and cliff tops offering ocean views. In April and November there is a good chance of seeing whales and perhaps sea lions. You are more likely, however, to be intrigued by chickadees and serenaded by white-crowned sparrows. One word of warning: the hike is well worth the effort, but the trail ends with a disappointing view.

By car, drive south from Netarts on the Three Capes Scenic Route. Pass the entrance to Cape Lookout State Park and follow the road upward. At 2½ miles stop at the overlook for a striking view north of Netarts Spit. About 3 miles from the park entrance find the well-marked Cape Lookout trailhead parking area.

Two trails leave from the far end of the parking lot. The right-hand trail, part of the Oregon Coast Trail, leads back to Cape Lookout State Park. Instead, take the trail directly behind the sign. At about 200 feet, pass a trail on the left side that switchbacks down to the southern beach. The cape trail continues straight ahead, descending gradually along the south side of the cape.

In about ½ mile a window in the trees gives a good view south. Nearby is a memorial to the crewmen of a World War II bomber that crashed against the cape in 1943. The wreckage was visible for many years but, fortunately, time and nature have covered the crash scar in the vegetation. At about 1¼ miles the trail dips into a saddle and climbs a few feet, switching from the south to the north side of the cape and offering a view down into the churning water of a cove.

From this point on, the trail switches sides a number of times with great views to the south. But there is not really a good view to the north anywhere along the trail. As you approach the end of the cape, the trail skirts the top of 400-foot-high cliffs. The hiker is sometimes protected by a steel cable for a handrail and sometimes by a solid-looking hedge of salal and huckleberries. The views are so dramatic that one is hard-pressed to know whether to watch where the feet are headed or to look at the view.

Close to the cape, the mournful sound of a foghorn located on a buoy becomes louder. The end of the trail is an anticlimax: it just ends against a wall of 10-foot-high salal, with views only to the south. We watched two local

Fishermen's path on Cape Lookout

fishermen descend a scary, 400-foot scramble trail to the water's edge. They said there were four whales here the week before. We suspect that to see whales the traveler should spend all day at the cape, as the fishermen had, not just a few minutes.

Hang gliders at Cape Kiwanda

20. SAND LAKE TO NESTUCCA BAY SPIT

Distance: 8 miles one way
  12 miles round trip
Hiking time: 4 hours one way
  6 hours round trip
Time of year: Any
Tide: Any
Obstacles: Headland to cross
Map: Tillamook County #2
  (Oregon Dept. of Transportation)

This 8 miles of sandy beach is broken only by beautiful Cape Kiwanda, certainly the fun capital of the Oregon coast. Great sport for the junior set is rolling and sliding down the steep sides of the biggest sand dune at the cape. If no one is watching such an undignified activity, some of the senior set might just be tempted to do the same.

Hang gliders soar in the prevailing wind, rising over the big sand dune that joins Cape Kiwanda to the mainland. The constant flow of air over the smooth sand here – unlike the gusts on many of the more rugged capes – makes this a favorite spot for soaring. With favorable winds the pilots can keep afloat for hours. The best view of the gliders is from the top of a sand dune.

From the community of Tierra Del Mar (south of the houses of Sand Lake) and its access road, hike northward 1 ½ miles to the Outlets River. From here, walk southward 4 miles along good beach to Cape Kiwanda. At the cape are a large parking lot and public restrooms.

A simple ascent to the top of the cape, with a gain of several hundred feet, may allow the traveler to see the hang gliders launching to the north. Don't try to walk around the cape – it's not possible.

As the traveler begins to drop down on the south side of Cape Kiwanda, a cross-trail leads up and out to the tip of the cape for an excellent view up and down the coast.

Another mile along the main trail brings the traveler to Pacific City, a substantial community with commercial campgrounds, motels, trailer courts, and boat launches. Here, in season, commercial fishermen launch 25-foot open fishing boats from trailers into the surf and out to sea. The launching generally occurs at daybreak. The boat motors are started onshore and the trailers are backed into the sea. The boats then roar off on the crest of the first breaker. Seldom, if ever, is the sea calm enough to make this launching a humdrum event.

While the return of the dories is not as breathtaking, it is still exciting to watch. The boats cruise along at a normal speed directly opposite their landing

Landing a fishing dory at Cape Kiwanda

spot. The pilot guns the motor and the boat, at full speed, jumps from wave to wave and coasts far up on the sandy beach.

From Pacific City, continue southward 3 miles down the spit that forms the west side of Nestucca Bay. It's a tantalizingly short distance from the end of the spit across the exit river to the opposite shore. To cross, you must beforehand arrange a ride either with a friendly fisherman or perhaps with the Nestucca Marina in Pacific City (503) 964-6410. Without arrangements for transportation, travelers will have to retrace their steps.

If you have only one vehicle but four or more people, you might consider splitting your party. Half the party can start at Tierra Del Mar and hike southward. The other half can move the vehicle to Pacific City and hike northward. An exchange of keys as you pass allows for easy transportation for all.

21. CAMP WINEMA (PORTER POINT) TO NESKOWIN

Distance: 4½ miles one way from Camp Winema
         5½ miles one way via Porter Point
Hiking time: 3 hours one way
Time of year: Any
Tide: Any
Obstacles: None
Map: Tillamook County #2
      (Oregon Dept. of Transportation)

This hike offers a long stretch of lonely beach and views of Nestucca Bay to the north and shaggy Cascade Head to the south. Drive southward from

Daley Lake and Kiwanda Beach

Kiwanda Beach

Pacific City for about 6 miles. Turn right on the side road leading to Camp Winema (look for signs). To the north of the camp is a public beach access. If you like, you can hike southward from here. But for a complete survey of this shore, hike northward one mile to Porter Point.

To the north, across the entrance to Nestucca Bay, lies Nestucca Spit and the sweep of beach that terminates in the playground of Cape Kiwanda. Adventurous hikers who want to cross over might be able to arrange a ride with a friendly fisherman or perhaps with the Nestucca Marina in Pacific City (503) 964-6410.

To the south looms the massive, green upthrust of Cascade Head. Walk south along the 4½ miles of excellent sandy beach. With the exception of Camp Winema and a few adjacent cottages, there is no civilization until the end of the hike, at Neskowin. About 3 miles south of Camp Winema, cross a small stream and continue until the beach ends at a cliff under Cascade Head. At one time a trail system crossed this head, but logging and regrowth has left a welter of unconnected and ill-defined game trails. Therefore, it is not recommended that you attempt to extend this hike over Cascade Head.

To reach Neskowin, backtrack and recross the stream, following the north bank upstream past a beautiful hotel/motel complex to a large state parking area. The closest campground is 6 miles up Neskowin Creek Road. Other accommodations are found at Pacific City.

Cascade Head trail

22. CASCADE HEAD TO THREE ROCKS
(Nature Conservancy Trail)

Distance: 2 miles one way
Hiking time: 1 hour
Time of year: Any
Tide: Any
Obstacles: None
Map: Tillamook County #2
     (Oregon Dept. of Transportation)

This dramatic Nature Conservancy Trail travels through wooded terrain to the top of Cascade Head. Then it descends, through open meadows with dramatic vistas to the south, to the tiny community of Three Rocks, on the Salmon River. This final descent loses 800 feet elevation. If you have only one vehicle, it is suggested that you begin the hike here to avoid having to make this climb on the return leg.

From Neskowin, drive U.S. 101 south to the crest of the hill and turn right (west) on Forest Service Road 1861. Drive 3 miles to the trailhead, which is marked by a Nature Conservancy sign and a white highway guardrail. Here you can pick up a Nature Conservancy brochure, which explains the ecology, geography, and the views along the way.

The first mile runs through woods along a fairly level, abandoned road to a vast grassy hillside. At this spot are great views over the mouth of the Salmon River and a striking low headland to the resort area of Lincoln City. The brochure explains how the Indians burned these headlands and the settlers grazed them, changing the vegetation from fields of lupine to ragwort, thistles, and several introduced species of grass.

In the mid-1960s, some local conservationists heard that the farmer who owned Cascade Head was proposing to sell the land to developers. As you sit and enjoy the view, you can be grateful that the farmer preferred selling his land to the Nature Conservancy, which bought it with money donated by hundreds of concerned citizens, including some corporations and developers often considered to be enemies of conservation.

From the summit, the way descends steeply through more meadows, losing 800 feet elevation before reaching the south trail head, at the small community of Three Rocks, on the Salmon River. Access to this point from U.S. 101 is via Three Rocks Road. A second turn to the right in about a mile is labeled "Nature Conservancy Trail."

Salmon River from Cascade Head

Chilwood Creek and Harts Cove

23. CASCADE HEAD TO HARTS COVE

Distance: 6 miles round trip
Hiking time: 3 hours
Time of year: Any
Tide: Any
Obstacles: Loss and gain of 600 feet
Map: Hebo (USGS)

This hike down to Harts Cove loses 600 feet of elevation, which must be regained on the return trip. You will probably not see another soul on this trip other than your companions. Large blocks of wild land extend north and south on this seaward side of Cascade Head. In both directions are impenetrable mazes formed of old logging cuts and crisscrossing animal trails.

For access to Cascade Head, follow the instructions in Hike 22. Passing the Nature Conservancy trailhead, continue on a dirt road, Forest Service Road 1861, for approximately one mile to the Harts Cove trailhead.

Winding downward through forest, the trail loses elevation rapidly for the first mile. Then, with ups and downs, it traverses the hillside, crossing first Cliff Creek, then Chitwood Creek. At times the trail is quite muddy and in other places steep, but the reward is being among the stately trees.

At approximately 3 miles, leave the old Cascade Head trail and drop into a large, grassy meadow with views of the rugged coastline to the south. With

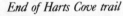

End of Harts Cove trail

binoculars, look at the offshore rocks, the source of the barking of sea lions. Follow the meadow down 200 feet to a point overlooking Harts Cove, a cliff-lined inlet of churning water. Chitwood Creek tumbles over a cliff into the cove. There is absolutely no way down to the water.

There are several good campsites near the top of the meadow. For most of the year, water can be found by following the now-abandoned Cascade Head trail another 500 feet to a small creek. If the creek is dry, go back in the direction of Chitwood Creek to the first spring.

Salmon River headland

24. ROADS END STATE PARK TO LINCOLN CITY

Distance: 6 miles
Hiking time: 3 hours
Time of year: Any
Tide: Any
Obstacles: None
Map: Lincoln County #1
      (Oregon Dept. of Transportation)

A mile-long sand bar, a beautiful headland, then miles of unbroken beach beckon the hiker here. However, the headland is on private property and the sand bar is only accessible by water.

At the north end of Lincoln City, by a large shopping center, leave U.S. 101 and follow signs one mile northward to the beach access at Roads End State Park. If you wish, hike the beach northward one mile until stopped by what locals call the Salmon River Headland. Try to time your hike to reach the headland at very low tide and explore the odd rock formations and tidal pools. Then head south 6 miles, passing Lincoln City, to reach the entrance of Siletz Bay.

The beach just past 2-mile-long Lincoln City is excellent hiking if you like lots of city life. After approximately 3 miles you pass a square, painted concrete fort of a hotel operated by a major chain. It would make an excellent prison or even a coastal defense fort if it fails as a hotel. Alongside it is a nice day center (with clean restrooms) maintained by the state of Oregon.

Continuing southward, you come to another "concrete fort" on a rather steep cliff. On the other side is a charming Spanish facade of arches and tile roofs. It's supposed to be very nice inside.

In ½ mile you round a headland to reach a small public park. Just beyond are several restaurants.

Accommodations are numerous in Lincoln City and campsites (including a hiker-biker camp) are available at Devils Lake State Park just north of the city.

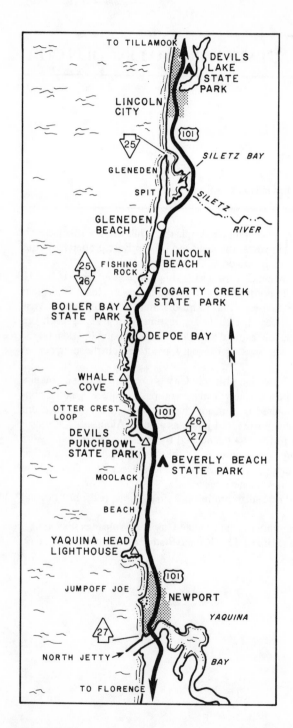

SECTION D.
Lincoln City to Newport

Walkable beaches, dramatic headlands, picturesque small towns, a lighthouse, and even a recent shipwreck give this section of the Oregon coast appeal for the hiker.

South of Lincoln City (see Hike 23), a large spit points northward from Gleneden Beach. From Gleneden Beach to Lincoln Beach is excellent hiking. But southward, the traveler is forced onto U.S. 101. A short network of trails extends out from Fogarty Creek, but ultimately the traveler will have to take a side route down to Boiler Bay.

Headlands where short hikes are possible continue down to the unusual community of Depoe Bay, which seems divided in two by a cleavage in a cliff. The highway at this point rises rather abruptly, then descends to the tiny community of Otter Rock.

Now, past the headlands, there is excellent beach hiking along the 5 miles of Beverly Beach to Yaquina Head, with its interesting lighthouse. Just south of Yaquina Head 3 miles of excellent beach extend past Jumpoff Joe and the town of Newport to terminate at the north jetty of Yaquina Bay. Here the traveler can look out at the remains of a wrecked Japanese freighter and search for traces of the 70,000-gallon oil and diesel spill.

There are bus stops at Lincoln City, Gleneden Beach, Depoe Bay and Newport. Campsites are available at Beverly Beach State Park; this route also offers many motels.

Beach near Fogarty Creek State Park

25. GLENEDEN SPIT TO FOGARTY CREEK STATE PARK

Distance: North, 6 miles round trip
           South, 3 miles one way
Hiking time: 5 hours
Time of year: Any
Tide: Any
Obstacles: Obscure trail exit
Map: Lincoln County #1
     (Oregon Dept. of Transportation)

Sandy, walkable beaches with a scattering of interesting homes nearby reward the hiker here. At the end of the trail, after a short climb to the top of a rock, one can enjoy views extending up and down the coast.

From Lincoln City it's ⅛ mile across the outlet of Siletz Bay to Gleneden Spit. It might be possible to hire a boat at Bailey's Moorage in Taft for this short trip. If so, you can enjoy a 6-mile, one-way hike south from the tip of Gleneden Spit to Fogarty Creek State Park.

Most hikers, however, will prefer to drive U.S. 101 southward past the famous resort of Salishan to the town of Gleneden Beach. Turn right on Laurel Street and drive to the end. There is a small parking area and a beach access road. The road crosses private property, but the beach is public domain.

From the parking lot, you can hike 3 miles northward over excellent beach, past many fine summer homes, to the end of the Gleneden Spit. While the spit appears stable, in fact a severe erosion problem has caused the loss of several homes. Note the extensive riprap in front of the remaining homes.

Southward from the Laurel Street parking area, the beach extends to just beyond the community of Lincoln Beach (not to be confused with Lincoln City) and terminates at the cliffs of Fishing Rock.

A scramble trail past the last house and the first cliff brings the traveler to the grassy top of Fishing Rock. Northward is a view of Cascade Head, to the south stands Government Point, and under the cliffs below is a pleasant little beach (not accessible from this location).

To reach the beach under the cliffs, drive to Fogarty Creek— ½ mile to the

south over First Rural Road and then U.S. 101. Fogarty Creek State Park is a pleasant day-use camp with a picnic ground to the east of the highway and a trail that passes under the highway bridge to reach the ocean beach.

26. FOGARTY CREEK STATE PARK TO DEVILS PUNCHBOWL

Distance: 10½ miles (including car travel)
Hiking time: 2 to 3 hours
Time of year: Any
Tide: Low at Boiler Bay
Obstacles: Some car travel
Map: Lincoln County #1
     (Oregon Dept. of Transportation)

This is a series of short hikes to tide pools full of marine life, scenic overlooks, and a pocket beach. Car travel is necessary.

Boiler from steam schooner J. Marhoffer

Entrance to Depoe Bay

First, park at Fogarty Creek State Park and follow the trail under the bridge to the beach. As the beach disappears against the cliffs, a trail takes the traveler up past Government Viewpoint and continues intermittently until it terminates at U.S. 101. Now retrace your steps to the starting point.

Next, drive to Boiler Bay, where there is a steep scramble trail down onto the rocky beach. Time your trip so you will arrive here at low tide, when you can explore fascinating tide pools. Here too is a rusting steam boiler, all that remains of the steam schooner *J. Marhoffer*, wrecked in 1910. The bay is a marine preserve, so look but do not collect.

Drive on to Depoe Bay, a small fishing and tourist town with a spectacular entrance to its harbor—a narrow slot between the two cliffs spanned by the highway bridge. Park on the seaward side and walk across the bridge to the south. Then cross the road (carefully, there is much traffic). From the bridge is a great view of the fishing harbor. Here the combination of a high tide and a southerly storm sends waves leaping skyward high above the highway.

Now drive on to Whale Cove, where there is a round-trip access to a pocket beach.

In another mile of driving, the highway splits. It is possible to travel, either on foot or by car, on the little-used, lower, old highway, which winds its way up past Cape Foulweather. After a gain of 400 vertical feet you'll arrive at

Otter Crest, where there is an excellent view both to the north and the south. Now the old road descends downhill.

A turn to the right will take you to Otter Rock and Devils Punchbowl State Park. The Punchbowl is known for its excellent tide pools, where marine life is protected. This spot must be dramatic at high tide during storms. A trail leads down from the north side of the parking area; some tourist shops are located here. The closest camp is 1½ miles to the south at Beverly Beach State Park. Motel accommodations are at Newport.

27. DEVILS PUNCHBOWL STATE PARK TO NEWPORT

Distance: 8 miles one way
Hiking time: 4 hours
Time of year: Any (May and June best for birdwatching)
Tide: Any
Obstacles: None
Map: Lincoln County #1
     (Oregon Dept. of Transportation)

This is a great bit of beach hiking past a lighthouse and a national wildlife refuge. The hike starts at Devils Punchbowl State Park, on Otter Rock. An

View from Devils Punch Bowl State Park

Beverly Beach State Park

access trail, altered by a 1982 slide, descends across from the public restrooms. Then a beautiful sandy beach extends past Beverly Beach State Park, with its campground, to Yaquina Head. If the tide is in, cross over Moolack Beach Rock.

Approximately 800 feet short of the Yaquina Head cliffs, an excellent trail rises to the community of Agate Beach. Yaquina Head may be passed by traveling a short distance southward on U.S. 101. Here, however, is an excellent one-mile side trip by road from U.S. 101 to the Yaquina Head lighthouse. En route is a mammoth gravel pit, a source of considerable frustration to Oregon's ecologists. The lighthouse, standing on a tall cliff, is all that a lighthouse should be. A few hundred feet northwest of the Yaquina Head lighthouse, on Right Island, are hundreds of nesting sea gulls, cormorants, and black and white common murres. The best time for viewing is May and June, before the chicks are old enough to fly. Bring your binoculars. All these offshore islands are part of the Oregon Coast National Wildlife Refuge.

Past Yaquina Head a gully leads from U.S. 101 to the beach. This section of the hike takes the traveler past the extended town of Newport, with its fascinating diversity of architecture. Here are 2 miles of excellent walking to the small bluff of Jumpoff Joe, which has considerably eroded since 1910 (see photo in the Marine Science Center). If the tide is in, cross the head by an access trail.

A mile farther south, the traveler reaches the north jetty of Yaquina Bay. Climb the stairway leading to Yaquina Bay State Park for a view of the remains of the 350-foot Japanese freighter *Blue Magpie*, which rammed the north jetty entrance while trying to enter the harbor during a storm in 1983. Seventy thousand gallons of oil and diesel fuel spilled. Two hundred seventy-four birds, including locally endangered brown pelicans, were killed. Many more were saved. While there is no oil spill damage visible to the casual viewer, the real, hidden damage is to marine life, particularly in Yaquina Bay—location of the Marine Science Center and a large fish hatchery. The Yaquina River is also the source of a substantial salmon run and has a large commercial fishing community.

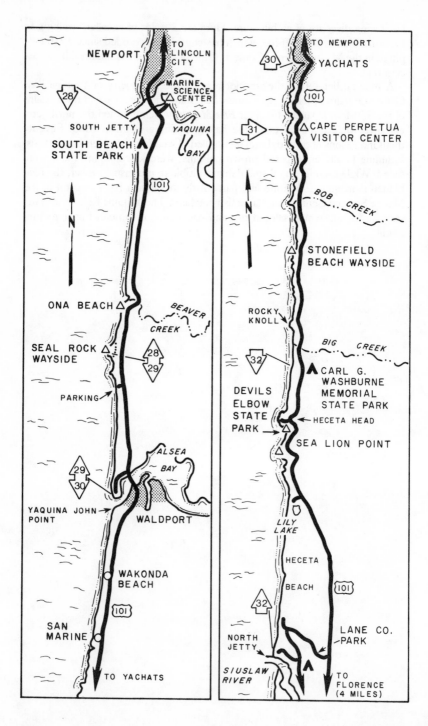

NEWPORT
TO LINCOLN CITY
MARINE SCIENCE CENTER
28
SOUTH JETTY
SOUTH BEACH STATE PARK
YAQUINA BAY
101
N
ONA BEACH
BEAVER CREEK
SEAL ROCK WAYSIDE
28
29
PARKING
ALSEA BAY
29
30
YAQUINA JOHN POINT
WALDPORT
WAKONDA BEACH
101
SAN MARINE
TO YACHATS

30
TO NEWPORT
YACHATS
101
31
CAPE PERPETUA VISITOR CENTER
BOB CREEK
N
STONEFIELD BEACH WAYSIDE
ROCKY KNOLL
BIG CREEK
32
CARL G. WASHBURNE MEMORIAL STATE PARK
DEVILS ELBOW STATE PARK
HECETA HEAD
SEA LION POINT
LILY LAKE
HECETA BEACH
101
32
LANE CO. PARK
NORTH JETTY
SIUSLAW RIVER
TO FLORENCE (4 MILES)

SECTION E.
Newport to Florence

Beach hiking is excellent from South Beach to Yachats, where the beaches disappear in steep cliffs. Inland from Waldport you'll find the trailhead for the Drift Creek Trails (see Hike 62).

Where U.S. 101 rounds Cape Perpetua there are excellent view points, small wayside hikes, and beach pools to explore. Now come several short hikes before Heceta Head, where the road winds treacherously past Sea Lion Point until the vast sweep of Heceta Beach, 7 miles long, comes into sight. This section terminates at the north jetty of the Siuslaw River, a few miles inland from Florence, in an area of many pocket beaches.

Although walking short stretches of highway is necessary for some of the hikes in this section, only the most dedicated will hike the highway its total length from Newport to Florence, particularly since winding roads and narrow shoulders present substantial danger from traffic.

Cape Creek at Cape Perpetua

Yaquina Head Lighthouse

28. YAQUINA BAY TO SEAL ROCK

Distance: 9½ miles one way
Hiking time: 5 hours
Time of year: Any
Tide: Any
Obstacles: None
Map: Lincoln County #2
       (Oregon Dept. of Transportation)

Between Newport and Waldport is a straightforward 15 miles of beach walking, with only Seal Rock Head to cross. For convenience, this stretch has been broken into two trips–Hike 28 and Hike 29.

Before starting, it would be a mistake to miss the Marine Science Display, which is located on the south side of Yaquina Bay, just to the east of the south buttress of the bridge. Drive past the boat launching ramps and parking places. An adequate tour of this display will require at least one hour. It is also an excellent place to photograph the great curved supports of the bridge, an Oregon coast trademark.

The hike starts from the south jetty, located just west of the bridge terminus at the little community of South Beach. Since the jetty is topped with a road that gets narrower, with no turnarounds, it is best to park and walk out. The ocean beach begins at the jetty and extends south – 7 miles of smooth sand. At low tide hundreds of ancient trees are exposed. They're held firmly in place by clay, rather than thrown to the high tide level, as are most drifting trees. Has the receding beach exposed an old lake bed?

Beaver Creek, at 8 miles, can be waded in summer. If the water is high, you cross to the highway and return to the beach through Ona Beach State Park. In another 1 ¼ mile you reach Seal Rock Head. Mountaineers may be tempted to climb up the steep sand to the top of the head. Because of the real danger of falling, however, this climb is not recommended. Just short of the rocks, ascend the scramble trail, which leads into the little community of Seal Rock. Here there is gasoline available and a general store. There are also an interesting vista and restrooms at Seal Rock Wayside. The closest campground is South Beach State Park, 6 miles back toward Newport. Motel accommodations are also available in Waldport to the south.

Logs that may have been covered since the Ice Age,
emerging from sand south of Newport

29. SEAL ROCK TO WALDPORT

Distance: 4 miles one way
Hiking time: 3 hours
Time of year: Any
Tide: Any
Obstacles: Access to beach obscured at both ends
Map: Lincoln County #2
      (Oregon Dept. of Transportation)

This hike features 4 miles of obstacle-free beach, which begins just south of Seal Rock Wayside. At the Waldport end you may have a bit of trouble finding the end of the beach access road.

From Seal Rock Wayside, descend southward over the trail to the rocks and pocket beach, where there are tide pools to explore. In ½ mile the beach ter-

Seal Rocks

minates in high rocks, forcing the traveler to return to the beginning. The next bend of coast must be rounded by car on the highway, since there is no way through without trespassing on private land.

To reach the north end of the 4-mile beach, follow U.S. 101 south from Seal Rock Wayside for ½ mile to the first major junction. Turn right and drive ⅛ mile to the beach. You will pass an immense chimney of an old burned-out lodge. If you wish, walk northward ¼ mile to the point. South from here the excellent sandy beach extends to the spit and the entrance to Alsea Bay, from where there is a view eastward of the immense Waldport Bridge. A tiny park at the end of the spit provides access to the roads of the resort community of Waldport. These roads lead slightly over a mile to a major junction with U.S. 101, just north of the bridge.

---

30. WALDPORT TO YACHATS

Distance: 8½ miles one way
Hiking time: 4 hours
Time of year: Any
Tide: Any
Obstacles: Rock-scrambling near Yachats
Map: Lincoln County #2
     (Oregon Dept. of Transportation)

This is a lovely beach hike on smooth sand. At the south end you must either scramble over some rocks or walk the highway into Yachats.

Ancient wreck at Big Creek

Yachats Bay

One-eighth mile south of the big highway bridge into Waldport, there is a cement bulkhead with a stairway down to the beach. Begin here if the tide is low. If the tide is high, continue another ⅛ mile on U.S. 101 and take the first right turn. Shortly thereafter, take the next turn down to the beach.

Walk around Yaquina John Point. For the next 8 miles there will be small scattered settlements such as Wakonda Beach and San Marine. The uplands become wet and marshy and the houses disappear at approximately 6 miles. The latter part of the trip is along a mostly deserted beach.

On the approach to Yachats the good beach quickly changes into a rocky headland, and you must scramble along broken rocks for the last ¾ mile to Yachats State Park. The only alternative at this point is to abandon the beach and follow a road to U.S. 101, which has wide shoulders leading into Yachats, a community of 700 to 800 people.

To the north of Yachats an Indian reservation was created in 1856 by the U.S. Government. An Indian Agency was located near the present site of the Yachats Cemetery. In this reservation were Indians from the Coos, Umpqua, Calapooga, Siuslaw and Alsea tribes. On September 16, 1875, the Yachats Reservation was closed; the Indians were officially moved to the Siletz Reservation and the land was opened for settlement. In theory the Indians could have availed themselves of the land, but they were hunters and fishermen, not farmers, so few stayed. There are no signs of the old reservation left to show man's inhumanity to man, but it is interesting to know a little of the history of this now-peaceful community.

31. CAPE PERPETUA VICINITY TRAIL HIKES

Distance: About 10 miles of trails
Hiking time: One day
Time of year: Any
Tide: Low tide is best
Obstacles: None
Maps: Cape Perpetua Area (U.S. Forest Service)

A good place to spend a day, Cape Perpetua offers an excellent interpretive center and a variety of short hiking trails. At the interpretive center you can view some extremely interesting illustrative displays, watch nature films, and

Devils Churn

pick up a descriptive brochure with trail information. To reach the center, drive south from Yachats around the spectacular nose of Cape Perpetua. You will pass a handsome house owned by a well known maritime writer. It looks like a lighthouse. The interpretive center is on a short, well-signed dead-end road above U.S. 101.

There are a series of access trails from several parking places below the interpretive center to the beach. There are not many tide pools on the Oregon coast, so this area is a special treat. Look, but do not touch. There will be others coming after you. It is possible at low tide to hike a crescent series of tide-pool rocks. It's also a place where the brave can jump from rock to rock and perhaps slip and become wet. Watch for sleeper waves. See the big-wave warning in the front of the book.

The 1½-mile Perpetua Trail leads to the top of Perpetua Head (also accessible by motor vehicle). Beginning at the top, a ½-mile interpretive loop circles the head. Along the loop are views from the south overlook and from the west shoulder, which looks to the north. The trail completes the loop through the Whispering Spruce Trail.

From the interpretive center, the mile-long Cape Cook Trail leads to the

Small tributary of Cape Creek

Harbor seal near Strawberry Hill Rest Area

Giant Spruce Trail. From the upper end of the parking lot exit the 1¼-mile loop of Riggin' Slinger Trail, a self-guided nature trail featuring forest management and ecology. A tape deck and script are available at the reception desk.

Captain Cook Ridge Trail adds 4 more round-trip miles through virgin forest to the nature trail. Hopefully, this will loop back to the Gwen Creek Trail in the near future.

The mile-long Cape Creek Trail leads to a very large, 500-year-old spruce. In season there bloom many wildflowers. Southward leads the Gwen Creek Trail, which eventually rounds Cape Cook Point and enters Neptune State Park, where a hiker-biker camp is located.

One-half mile beyond Neptune State Park, there is a small rest area at Strawberry Hill. This section is popular with a large number of seals, who like to sleep on small off-shore islands. Binoculars would be desirable here.

Immediately after rounding the cape there is a parking lot. An eighth of a mile hike back will bring you to a good view down into the leaping and dancing waters of the appropriately named Devil's Churn. It's not accessible by foot.

Apparently, an old unpaved road extends southward for several miles from the visitor's center. Ask the ranger for information as to access and egress.

View from Perpetua Head

South by vehicle a short distance is Stonefield Beach State Wayside, where the graves of 3-year-old Katie Myrth Bray and Georgiania Starr Bray are located. The Bray family farmed in this locale long before the first road was built between Yachats and Florence, in 1913. The only way the Bray family could reach their farm was by walking on the beach and along trails, much as coast hikers do now.

Southward along Sea Rose Beach is a scattering of old motels. There are also a series of small beaches to explore. A large campground is located at Carl G. Washburne Memorial State Park, 2½ miles to the south.

32. CARL G. WASHBURNE MEMORIAL STATE PARK TO FLORENCE

Distance: 15 miles one way (7½ miles of hiking)
Hiking time: 3½ hours
Time of year: Any
Tide: Low tide is better
Obstacles: Inconvenient access
Map: Lane County #1
      (Oregon Dept. of Transportation)

Included here is a short beach hike north of Heceta Head and, to the south, a wonderful 6-mile hike on Heceta Beach. Connecting the two is one of the more spectacular sections of highway along the Oregon coast.

Heceta Head Lighthouse

The first section of this hike starts at Carl G. Washburne Memorial State Park (11 miles south of Yachats, 14 miles north of Florence). Hike southward 2 miles on the beach until the cliffs start rising toward Heceta Head. At this point, you can turn back or, if you have arranged a car shuttle, look sharply for the trail that climbs ¼ mile to U.S. 101. There is a parking lot at this point.

To reach the trailhead for Heceta Beach, follow U.S. 101 southward from the parking lot. The highway climbs 350 feet over Heceta Head, then descends in a steep switchback past Heceta Head Lighthouse. Devils Elbow State Park (day use only) is down a steep road leading to the mouth of Cape Creek. The highway passes above the creek on a high bridge and plunges into a narrow tunnel, emerging on a shelf carved in a near-vertical cliff – an excellent place to park. The retaining wall holding the highway in place is an impressive example of the Oregon Highway Department's engineering skills. A telephoto lens is desirable for photographing Heceta Head Lighthouse to the north.

Sea Lion cave

A short distance farther along is the entrance to Sea Lion Caves. This commercial venture charges a fee to descend in an elevator to several small caves and a huge grotto where, during winter months, hundreds of sea lions gather. The highway winds on until a magnificent sweeping view appears of Heceta Beach to the south. Park here, on the ocean side of U.S. 101.

A small scramble trail leads down to the beach through gorse, a thick bush with sharp inhospitable spines. Garden shears would be most desirable to assist in opening this scramble trail. As an alternative, wear heavy, thorn-proof clothing. Or you might prefer to continue on the highway to the first major turn to the right, which leads ¾ mile to the beach, past Lily Lake, Lily Lake Stream, and Sutton Creek. Where the streams enter the ocean, high tides, particularly in winter, can make beach access difficult or impossible. At low tides, both creeks fan out and can be crossed.

Head south along the beach. At 4½ miles appears Heceta Beach, a resort/retirement community with one excellent motel. At 5½ miles, you reach a parking lot at the north jetty of the Siuslaw River. Here a paved road leads a short mile to Lane County Park, which has an excellent campground. From the jetty, it is 5 miles along the Siuslaw River into the thriving town of Florence.

California pitcher (Darlingtonia californica), *an insect-trapping plant found near Florence*

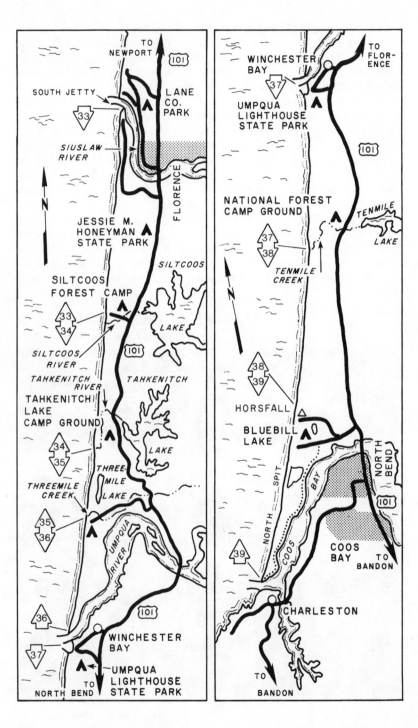

TO
NEWPORT 101

SOUTH JETTY

LANE
CO.
PARK

33

SIUSLAW
RIVER

N

FLORENCE

JESSIE M.
HONEYMAN
STATE PARK

SILTCOOS

SILTCOOS
FOREST CAMP

33
34

LAKE

101

SILTCOOS
RIVER

TAHKENITCH
RIVER

TAHKENITCH

TAHKENITCH
LAKE
CAMP GROUND

34
35

LAKE

THREE-
MILE
LAKE

THREEMILE
CREEK

35
36

UMPQUA
RIVER

36

101

WINCHESTER
BAY

37

UMPQUA
LIGHTHOUSE
STATE PARK

TO
NORTH BEND

WINCHESTER
BAY

TO
FLOR-
ENCE

37

UMPQUA
LIGHTHOUSE
STATE PARK

101

NATIONAL FOREST
CAMP GROUND

TENMILE
LAKE

37
38

TENMILE
CREEK

N

38
39

HORSFALL

BLUEBILL
LAKE

NORTH
BEND

COOS
BAY

NORTH SPIT

101

39

COOS
BAY

TO
BANDON

CHARLESTON

TO
BANDON

SECTION F.
Florence to North Bend (Oregon Dunes National Recreation Area)

The Oregon Dunes National Recreational Area is divided into two sections. The northern section terminates in a spit at the north jetty of the Umpqua River, not far from Winchester Bay. The southern section runs from Winchester Bay to Coos Bay North Spit. These two sections contain nearly 40 miles of long, smooth beaches for easy hiking. Between the beaches and U.S. 101 is a strip of rolling sand dunes several miles wide. Only occasional trails or roads lead out to the beach, and careful route-finding is in order. Unfortunately for the hiker, vehicles are allowed on the beaches most of the time.

Each of these sections would make good two- to three-day backpacking excursions. Extreme care should be taken to purify stream water.

The sand dunes are not the only spectacular attraction of the Oregon Dunes—the lakes and streams and forest are all worth exploring. There is a surprising variety of vegetation, from the pioneer grasses and flowers that are nature's way of stabilizing the shifting sand, to the forest-covered dunes with their dense ground cover of evergreen huckleberry, 10-foot-high salal, and tree-sized rhododendrons, which bloom in late May. Behind the large dunes are often found marshes with huge skunk cabbages, Labrador tea, and Darlingtonia, with its strangely shaped leaves that catch and digest bugs.

Wind patterns

33. SIUSLAW RIVER TO SILTCOOS

Distance: 10 miles one way
Hiking time: 5 hours
Time of year: Any
Tide: Any (better if low)
Obstacles: Off-road vehicles
Map: Oregon Dunes National Recreational Area contour map

On this hike you'll stride along 10 miles of sand, edged by dunes rising several hundred feet.

Beyond Florence and the Siuslaw River Bridge, U.S. 101 rises 0.7 mile to a right turn onto the South Jetty Road. After traveling through scanty development and pines for several miles, the road turns 4 miles northward to reach the south jetty of the Siuslaw River. Here the Greenpeace Foundation has erected a memorial to 41 sperm whales who beached themselves and died here on June 16, 1979 – an occurrence which scientists have yet to understand.

The hike begins at the south jetty, where there is beach access. To the south extend 10 miles of long, smooth, flat sand, without homes or other developments. It is the sort of beach where the traveler can move rapidly – and get sore feet. To the east, sand dunes covered with scanty vegetation rise several hundred feet. These dunes, with their tiny pothole lakes, form a wilderness area containing small mammals, birds, and ocean grasses. Glaucous gulls wheel; sandpipers run in formation, dipping their long pointed bills in the receding surf to consume microscopic organisms.

The beach comes to an abrupt end at the Siltcoos River, which is substantial enough so that you will not be tempted to wade. Just inland from the beach is a parking area at the end of the Siltcoos River Road. This access road is well marked on U.S. 101. A bridge over the Siltcoos River leads shortly to a small drive-in campground, popular with the off-road vehicle people because of a beach access immediately to the south of the river.

The Siltcoos River Road turnoff is 7 miles south of the Siuslaw River Bridge in Florence. From the turnoff, drive west 1½ to 2 miles to the beach.

Mouth of the Siuslaw River

34. SILTCOOS RIVER TO TAHKENITCH RIVER

Distance: 5 miles one way
Hiking time: 2½ hours
Time of year: Any
Tide: Any
Obstacles: Difficult access at south end; off-road vehicles
Map: Oregon Dunes National Recreation Area contour map

It is possible to walk from the Siltcoos River to the Tahkenitch River and from there out to Tahkenitch Lake Campground just off U.S. 101. However, *from the beach* the trail leading to the campground is difficult to find. It would be desirable for Forest Service officials to establish a line of posts across the approximately ½-mile stretch of sand from the beach to the beginning of the trail in the vegetation. As it is, Pacific winds and shifting sands regularly obliterate any footprints or signs of access. It is, accordingly, recommended that you follow this trail *out to* the beach and hike this stretch of shore from south to north.

Crossing Tahkenitch River in Oregon Dunes National Recreation Area

The Tahkenitch Lake Campground is located on the right (west), 13 miles south of the turnoff from U.S. 101 to the south jetty of the Siuslaw River. The campground is small, with primitive restrooms. From there the trail leads a short mile over the vegetation-covered sand dunes down to the beach. After a very pretty stretch wandering through scrub pines, the trail comes to a large expanse of sand across which the Pacific Ocean and beaches are clearly visible. You should reach the beach just south of the Tahkenitch River. However, if the wind has cleansed the sand of footprints, getting to the beach may require a degree of skill in navigation—even after the river is located.

Across the easily waded Tahkenitch River, 4½ miles of easy, flat, smooth, hard beach stretch northward to the Siltcoos River. To the east lie rolling dunes devoid of habitation. At the Siltcoos River, a short off-road vehicle trail leads up into a comfortable campground that, unfortunately for the hiker, is favored by the dune-buggy crew. Even so, it is a good place to camp (for access, see Hike 33).

35. TAHKENITCH LAKE CAMPGROUND TO THREEMILE CREEK

Distance: 5 miles one way
Hiking time: 2 hours
Time of year: Any
Tide: Any
Obstacles: Difficult access
Map: Oregon Dunes National Recreational Area contour map

A wildlife sanctuary among the rolling dunes and a dense forest of conifers are among the attractions of this beach hike.

However, both ends of this hike have difficult access problems. The Tahkenitch Lake Campground is located on the right, 13 miles south of the turnoff from U.S. 101 to the south jetty of the Siuslaw River. It is a small campground, with primitive restrooms. From this campground a trail leads up over the vegetation-covered sand dunes and down to the beach (see Hike 34). It is a short mile from the campground to the ocean. Turning southward, you walk 5 miles to reach Threemile Creek. To the left is a wildlife sanctuary of rolling, partially grass-clad sand dunes with an occasional pond. Beyond this

Pond surrounded by sand dunes near Eel Creek Campground

Sand dunes engulfing forest near Eel Creek Campground,
Oregon Dunes National Recreation Area

half-mile-wide margin rises a dense, green, coniferous forest unblighted by human hand. It's a good place to escape from civilization—unless you have the misfortune of meeting a 4-wheel-drive vehicle. At 4½ miles, look sharply to the left for the 4-wheel-drive road exiting onto the beach (if you reach the stream, you've gone too far). If the road is not visible, hike upstream along Threemile Creek to the vegetation and explore northward until you locate the road.

Access to this road from U.S. 101 is at the crest above the Umpqua River Basin—take Douglas County Road 247. This excellent dirt road with overhanging trees deteriorates as it winds downhill. The split in the road is simply the division of good and bad roads, both of which are now bad. This junction is a good place to park unless you have a 4-wheel-drive vehicle. Threemile Creek would be an excellent place to camp, provided the water is properly purified.

Three Mile Lake, Oregon Dunes National Recreation Area

36. THREEMILE LAKE AND THREEMILE CREEK TO THE UMPQUA RIVER

Distance: 10 miles round trip
Hiking time: 3½ hours
Time of year: Any
Tide: Any
Obstacles: Difficult route to beach
Map: Oregon Dunes National Recreational Area contour map

This is a round-trip hike to the Umpqua River north jetty. It begins at a good place to camp where there is a nearby side trip—an opportunity to explore Threemile Lake.

Approximately 17 miles south of Florence, U.S. 101 sharply crests above the Umpqua River Basin. Turn right on Douglas County Road 247. This gravel and dirt road winds down the hill, with overhanging trees, with the road gradually deteriorating. The split in the road is simply a division of good and bad roads, both of which are now bad. This junction is an excellent place to camp and backpack the ½ mile to the beach. There is also good camping in the vicinity of Threemile Creek, provided the water is carefully purified.

From here, there are 5 miles of excellent beach walking on the mile-wide, south-extending peninsula of sand that forms the north bank of the Umpqua River. On gaining the jetty, at the tip of this peninsula, the Coast Guard light-house is clearly visible, as is the small town of Winchester Bay to the east. It might be possible ahead of time to hire a boat at Winchester Bay to take you across to the north jetty, thereby avoiding a 10-mile round trip.

Threemile Lake is approximately one mile north of Threemile Creek. There is no trail to the lake, which extends in a north-south direction. The first low dunes you cross are covered with sharp spearlike grass. You then skirt some swamps that push through a line of low spruce trees into the wind-eroded plain of open sand. At the top of the ridge, the traveler (if lucky) will be looking down at Threemile Lake. The map shows two lakes with a total length of 1 ½ miles. However, the two lakes appear to be one body of water with an hourglass shape. The lake's coffee-colored water is caused by natural vegetable dyes. If you take care on your approach, you may be rewarded by the sight of numerous birds, and perhaps deer. In season there is a great variety of flowers.

37. WINCHESTER BAY TO TENMILE CREEK

Distance: 9 ½ miles one way
Hiking time: 4 ½ hours
Time of year: Spring through fall
Tide: Any
Obstacles: Major stream crossing; route-finding problem at the end
Maps: Oregon State Forestry, North Unit
Coos Forest Protection District

A lighthouse marks the beginning of this hike along smooth sand; arrival at a quick-flowing creek completes it.

From the town of Winchester Bay, proceed west on Salmon Harbor Drive – past the boat basin, past the whaler exhibit, past recreation vehicles – to the peculiar, triangular south jetty of the Umpqua River and the start of this hike. The original Umpqua Lighthouse was erected at this site in 1847. Floods destroyed it in 1861. The present lighthouse, built in 1892, sits above the jetty. It is accessible by road, but not open to the public. This classic lighthouse is 67 feet tall, with a 1,800,000 candle-power light visible for 18 to 20 miles.

At this point, you have two choices: (1) to continue driving down the road behind the dunes for approximately 3 miles and begin hiking from there, or (2) to cross over onto the beach—which is straight, flat, and smooth—and start hiking immediately.

It is approximately 8 miles to Tenmile Creek. Just beyond the creek is a jeep road (described in Hike 38) which goes 2 miles out to the highway. If the creek is impassable, it is possible to follow it upstream on the north side over soft, slow sand. The best alternative, however, is to return to Winchester Bay. If you follow Tenmile Creek, it will take at least 1½ hours to reach U.S. 101. A very attractive campground (excellent for tent camping) is located on the north side of Tenmile Creek just west of U.S. 101.

Umpqua Lighthouse

Tenmile Creek near Spinreel Campground

38. TENMILE CREEK TO HORSFALL

Distance: 11 miles one way
Hiking time: 5 hours
Time of year: Any
Tide: Any
Obstacles: Windblown sand may obscure exits
Maps: Oregon State Forestry, North Unit
　　　　 Coos Forest Protection District

This hike allows you to meander through sand dunes, under wind-contorted trees, and past sparkling small ponds and lakes. Commonly seen are the paw prints of small animals, tracks of birds—and, quite possibly, the makers of these marks in the sand. After reaching the beach at Tenmile Creek, follow

123

the smooth, sandy beach for the rest of a pleasant journey.

From U.S. 101, turn east at Tenmile settlement. Turn immediately right on Wildwood Drive, proceeding under U.S. 101 to Spinreel Campground (excellent for tenting). A jeep trail goes immediately out the rear of the camp approximately 2 miles to the beach. The trail, sandy and unmarked, goes over the hills to a large lake and skirts around the lake to the north. Pass a less-used junction to the right; the true trail continues on. Follow the most-used tracks beyond the lake. The trail winds through the trees and eventually drops down into a large round delta just south of Tenmile Creek. (If this hike is done in reverse, the jeep road is approximately ⅛ to ¼ mile south of Tenmile Creek.) Because of the multitude of off-road vehicle tracks, this section can be confusing.

Turn south. The next 9 miles are over smooth, easily traveled sand. In the beginning, green hills are visible in the interior of the dunes area. Soon the view of hills is blocked by the dunes. On one trip, the author's party met large colonies of gulls, which would fly up when approached, circle downward, and land again. After this was repeated three or four times, they tired of being chased and flew slowly northward into the wind.

From the beach, Cape Arago is visible in the distance. The Horsfall parking lot, not visible from the beach, is hiding behind the row of dunes. The only indication it's there is a sign and some windblown jeep tracks coming over the bluff. Since the bluff is pierced in a number of places by jeep tracks, when in doubt look over to see if there is a large paved parking lot on the other side. Road access to Horsfall is described in Hike 39.

Left: *Osprey and nest near Tenmile Creek, Oregon Dunes National Recreation Area.* Below: *Tenmile Creek flowing past sand dunes*

39. HORSFALL TO COOS BAY NORTH SPIT

Distance: 9½ miles one way
Hiking time: 4 hours
Time of year: Any
Tide: Any
Obstacles: Access routes difficult to find
Maps: Oregon State Forestry, North Unit
　　　Coos Forest Protection District

The chances of meeting an off-road vehicle here are offset by the pleasant hiking down the broad, easy-to-walk beach of North Spit. The beach appears to lead directly into the city of North Bend, which looms closer and closer until the Coos River terminates the hike.

Access to Horsfall is over a causeway, located ½ mile north of the bridge over Coos Bay into the community of North Bend. The causeway leads in a southwesterly direction toward lumber mills. Pay sharp attention to the local sign directing you to Horsfall Access Road. This road may be closed by a gate during the winter. Alternatively, the road may be closed a short distance farther on by high water. Don't attempt to drive across. Skirting the water, walk out approximately one mile to the paved parking lot. There is a nice campground with good tent camping–popular with the off-road vehicle folks.

It is 7 miles from Horsfall down the beach to the north jetty. As in the preceding hikes, the sand is smooth and permits easy walking. You will have the usual escort of glaucous gulls. To the south you may see a large freighter loaded with logs passing through the entrance of Coos Bay. To the left is a margin of rolling sand dunes blocking the view across this peninsula to industrial activities on the bay (there are several sawmills). Again the beach is open to four-wheel-drive vehicles. My personal prejudice is that beaches are for feet, not wheels.

There are several methods of return from the jetty. A jeep road coming from the end of the jetty parallels the beach, just behind the dunes. The road swings southward along the margin of a substantial lake; it then emerges on pavement. A second jeep road comes across to the pavement on the north side of the same lake.

Alternatively, an abandoned jeep road goes up the east side of the spit. Located along this road are some World War II ammunition storage bunkers. A dilapidated wooden building is the site of an old Coast Guard rescue center. Continuing on, the road ends near Oregon Aqua Foods, Inc., where a mostly paved, sometimes gravel road leads outward past the mills. There is a distinct jog across the railroad tracks just to the east of one large mill. For traffic coming the other direction, a sign prohibits entry into the mill. Simply jog to the left here.

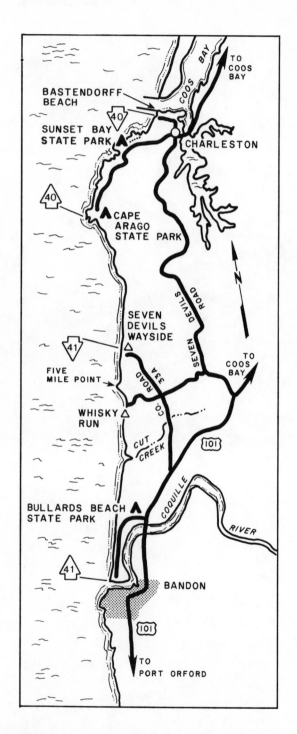

BASTENDORFF BEACH

SUNSET BAY STATE PARK

40

COOS BAY

TO COOS BAY

CHARLESTON

40

CAPE ARAGO STATE PARK

SEVEN DEVILS ROAD

N

SEVEN DEVILS WAYSIDE

41

FIVE MILE POINT

CO. ROAD 33A

TO COOS BAY

WHISKY RUN

CUT CREEK

101

BULLARDS BEACH STATE PARK

COQUILLE

RIVER

41

BANDON

101

TO PORT ORFORD

SECTION G.
North Bend to Bandon

The coastline between North Bend, on Coos Bay, and Bandon, at the mouth of the Coquille River, begins in city streets. A series of pocket beaches follows, terminating in the high overlook of Cape Arago. To the south are the Seven Devils, seven rolling ridges running in a generally east-west direction. They terminate in cliffs above the ocean. There are no safe beaches nor established trails in this area. You should "hike" this area with your eyes, not your feet. From Seven Devils Wayside, wide, sandy beaches extend to the Coquille River north jetty. U.S. 101 swings inland between North Bend and Bandon, so it is necessary to drive secondary roads for coastal access.

Four miles north of the Coquille River, the steamship *Tacoma*, loaded with 3500 tons of coal en route from Tacoma to San Francisco, was lost in 1882. This shipwreck took the lives of 10 people. John Bergman organized a volunteer crew and saved the remaining passengers. He received a gold hero's medal, and later became the keeper of a livesaving station. In 1892, the whaleback *Wetmore*, an odd-looking vessel—like a submarine with a catwalk on top—came to an end without loss of life, in heavy fog, one mile north of the Coquille River entrance.

In September of 1918, the $2 million ocean liner *Congress* was lost to fire 3 miles off Coos Bay. All 423 aboard were saved. The vessel was rebuilt and served safely for years thereafter. In November, 1910, the cargo steamship *Czarina*, while crossing the bar at Coos Bay, was thrown by tremendous swells onto the North Spit. Only one of the 25 crew members survived. In November, 1915, the S.S. *Santa Clara* was lost to an uncharted shoal near Coos Bay, and in 1943, YMS-133 (a World War II product) was likewise lost on the Coos Bay bar—16 saved, 13 lost. It is not hard to understand the need for jetties to tame the Coos River.

Ship on Coos Bay

40. BASTENDORFF BEACH (Charleston) TO CAPE ARAGO

Distance: 8 miles one way (4 miles of hiking)
Hiking time: 2 hours
Time of year: Any
Tide: Any
Obstacles: None
Map: Coos County #1
     (Oregon Dept. of Transportation)

There is a lot of variety in this drive-and-hike – a short beach, an interesting parade of homes, and a four-mile trail with great views.

Leaving U.S. 101 at Coos Bay, take the side road heading southwest to the pretty little community of Charleston. You may prefer to stroll the streets of this quiet, picturesque town rather than drive by. Bastendorff Beach County Park, the start of our hike, is located near the south jetty. Ahead is Yoakam Point, a short section of beach that terminates in a cliff, and a trail inland to the road. You are within the sound of the surf of Lighthouse Beach. Unfortunately, visibility is obscured by a line of homes, as is access to the beach. The variety of architectural design, evidencing local ingenuity, somewhat compensates for the loss of view. Unfortunately, the Coast Guard has fenced off access to the Cape Arago Lighthouse and its view point.

Ahead 1 ½ miles is Sunset Bay State Park, with campsites available. You can obtain a view of the lighthouse from the boat launch at the north end of Sunset Bay parking area. To reach it, follow the trail above the bluff a short ½ mile. A telephoto lens and binoculars would be desirable.

Cape Arago Lighthouse

Cape Arago State Park

From the south end of the Sunset Bay parking lot, a well-developed 4-mile trail alternates between forest and spectacular views of surf crashing on the rugged shoreline. The park rangers can supply a map showing this trail. Frequently, the distinctive sea lions' bark carries from the off-shore island. Along the way there is an occasional pocket beach.

From the upper end of the picnic area, a service road leads to a hiker-biker campground. There are motels and other accommodations in Charleston.

Charleston

41. SEVEN DEVILS WAYSIDE TO COQUILLE RIVER LIGHTHOUSE

Distance: 8 miles one way
Hiking time: 4 hours
Time of year: Any
Tide: Any
Obstacles: None
Map: Coos County #1
　　　(Oregon Dept. of Transportation)

Immediately south of the Seven Devils — seven ridges of dense brush without a trail — there lies a beautiful, sandy beach that will thrill the hiker. In the

Coquille River Lighthouse

south it ends at Bullards Beach State Park, immediately north of Bandon. This beach has a history of shipwrecks and a modern version of wealth: energy.

The Seven Devils Road runs from Charleston to an intersection with U.S. 101, 3 miles north of Bandon. The easiest, most certain access is to proceed north from Bandon on U.S. 101, then turn left onto the Seven Devils Road. (The map shows a shorter route for travelers coming south from Coos Bay, but the way given here is surer.) Drive 4½ miles to a sign pointing toward Seven Devils Wayside, on the right, a short ½-mile drive down to the beach. Here is an excellent parking lot at sea level. At the beginning of the hike, a few homes sit on the bluff high above the beach, facing seaward. The next group of houses is at Five Mile Point, but there your attention will be caught by a very large windmill, the Whisky Run Wind Turbine, owned by Pacific Power & Light Company. Its large, thick blades make an 80-foot-diameter circle on top of a high tower. With 30 miles per hour of wind, it produces 200 kilowatts of electricity.

Whisky Run Wind Turbine

Seven Devils Beach from Whisky Run Point

Five Mile Point can be rounded at three-quarter tide or scrambled over. After another ½ mile you arrive at Whisky Run Creek, where in 1853, 2,000 miners worked an extremely rich gold deposit. Misfortune came in 1854, when, in a violent storm, shifting sand buried the deposit beyond hope of recovery. As the hike proceeds southward the high bank diminishes to sand dunes. The last 1½ miles is a spit, the scene of many shipping disasters (recounted in the Section G introduction). The shipwrecks led to the creation of the north jetty at the end of this hike. Here, near a parking lot, a small lighthouse is an excellent subject for photography.

The whole area is part of well-groomed Bullards Beach State Park. Here is a day picnic area and, more importantly to the camper, an excellent, sheltered camping area. The closest motels are in Bandon.

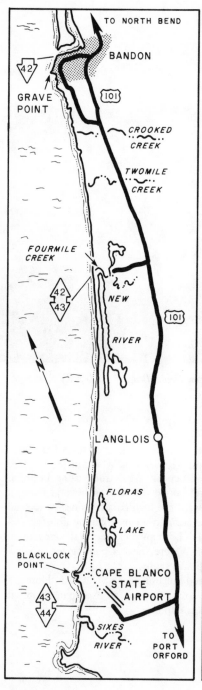

TO NORTH BEND

BANDON

42

GRAVE
POINT

101

CROOKED
CREEK

TWOMILE
CREEK

FOURMILE
CREEK

42
43

NEW

RIVER

101

N

LANGLOIS

FLORAS

LAKE

BLACKLOCK
POINT

43
44

CAPE BLANCO
STATE
AIRPORT

SIXES
RIVER

TO
PORT
ORFORD

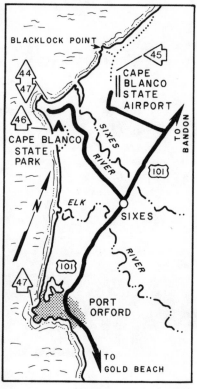

BLACKLOCK POINT

45

44
47

CAPE
BLANCO
STATE
AIRPORT

46

CAPE BLANCO
STATE
PARK

SIXES
RIVER

TO
BANDON

101

N

ELK

SIXES

47

RIVER

101

PORT
ORFORD

TO
GOLD BEACH

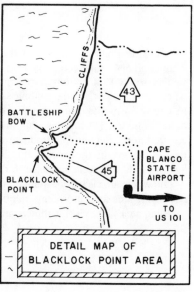

CLIFFS

43

BATTLESHIP
BOW

CAPE
BLANCO
STATE
AIRPORT

BLACKLOCK
POINT

45

TO
US 101

DETAIL MAP OF
BLACKLOCK POINT AREA

SECTION H.
Bandon to Port Orford

While U.S. 101 runs in almost a straight line between these two cities, the terrain to the west of the highway is quite remote. In fact, it would make an excellent four- or five-day backpacking trip. The first section, from Bandon south to Fourmile Creek, is rather civilized. Beyond that, a large lake blocks access to the east. Thereafter a wild area requires careful route finding. Near Cape Blanco, a ship's prow of rock can be rounded only at extreme low tide. Slippery rocks lead to a climb over the wild area of Blacklock Point. Ahead lies Cape Blanco, and beyond that, a long beach to Port Orford. Three major streams must be crossed en route.

Again, hikers are reminded to exercise great care when walking along the southern Oregon coast, where high tides obliterate beaches, and waves smash the abutting cliffs. These dangers exist year-round, but especially in winter, when tides are higher and seas often stormy. Be sure to consult a tide table before planning your trip. And listen to weather reports so that you don't get caught on a beach during a major storm.

Bandon Needles

42. BANDON TO FOURMILE CREEK

Distance: 8½ miles one way
Hiking time: 4 hours
Time of year: Any
Tide: Any
Obstacles: None
Map: Bandon (USGS)

This hike starts in the city of Bandon amongst some of the most spectacular rock needles on the Oregon coast, then passes on to miles of wide, sandy beaches, uninhabited except for birds that nest in marshes behind the 500-foot-wide sand dunes. The hike ends at Fourmile Creek, for which driving directions are given in Hike 43.

In Bandon, either walk or drive along the south side of the harbor to the south jetty and head south.

The south jetty has an interesting history. In 1953, the 307-foot freighter *Oliver Olson* struck the south jetty rocks. The quarter-million-dollar vessel was ultimately declared a total loss. Later, when the jetty was extended, the upper part of the hull was cut away, filled with rocks, and incorporated into the jetty, where it remains today. It might be possible to see the hull's rusted plates by peeking between the jetty rocks.

From the jetty, head south, crossing over Coquille Point on city streets. At high tide, follow the street along the bluff and return to the beach at Graves Point. If the tide permits, drop back to the beach and walk among the famous Bandon needles. At approximately one mile, round Graves Point.

The way opens up to a wide, sandy beach stretching out into the haze. At first there are people and houses in sight, but soon Bandon is left behind. By Crooked Creek, the parallel road disappears and U.S. 101 lies several miles inland. The bluff recedes, leaving a "wasteland" to the left. But what a wasteland—a rolling terrain of sand dunes capped with marsh grass and sprinkled with occasional pocket ponds, several small lakes, and a natural wildlife sanctuary for ducks, sea gulls, and small mammals. All this is topped off in April by acres of bright yellow gorse.

Bandon Needles

At 8½ miles from the south jetty you reach Fourmile Creek. Here, turn inland to Lower Fourmile Creek Road – only a few hundred feet away. Backpackers will want to cross the stream and hike another ½ mile away from civilization before camping. See Hike 43 concerning the stream crossing.

43. FOURMILE CREEK TO CAPE BLANCO STATE AIRPORT

Distance: 12 miles one way
Hiking time: 6 hours
Time of year: Late spring to early fall
Tide: Any
Obstacles: River crossing
Maps: Bandon, Langlois, Cape Blanco (USGS)
        Coos County #2, Curry County #1
        (Oregon Dept. of Transportation)

Read the Southern Oregon Coast Warning in the introduction, "What You'll Need to Know."

This hike is on a long, straight, sandy spit with the New River (a lake) on one side and the ocean on the other. At the start there is a stream crossing to contend with and at the end, some route problems in reaching the Cape Blanco State Airport, formerly called Curry County Airport.

From Bandon, drive U.S. 101 7½ miles south to the Lower Fourmile Creek Road (if you reach the Upper Fourmile Creek Road, you have gone too far). The road is well signed, but there is very little warning, so watch the miles carefully. Follow the road westward to its end in a new subdivision, within sight of the beach. In 1982, there was no problem crossing from the road to the beach, but this could change when the property is sold. The road access to the airport is described in Hike 44.

Upon reaching the beach, one is immediately confronted with crossing Fourmile Creek – virtually impossible in the winter months or after a major storm. Fourmile Creek drains a large area, including Floras, Croft and New lakes. After a week or more of rain the creek becomes a substantial river, requiring ropes and experience to cross – not a task for the unskilled. (See general information on stream crossings in the introduction.) However, during the summer months the creek can easily be waded at medium to low tide.

Across the creek, the way follows a 6-mile-long sand spit between New River and the ocean, a spit that may be breached by giant waves during a major storm. Occasionally an inaccessible farmhouse can be seen in the distance across the river. As Floras Lake comes into view, abandoned telephone poles without wires march like sentries down the crest of the adjacent shoulder and down a steep sand bank.

Looking far down the beach, you may be able to see the Cape Blanco Lighthouse and, in the evening, the flashing lights of the airport.

At approximately 10 miles there is a possible campsite at the mouth of a distinct cleavage in the bank, which usually has a small stream flowing through it. Immediately south of the cleavage, on a prominent nose, a footworn trail runs up a low sandbank. Visible to the left of the nose is a road, an alternate exit to the top of the bluff. Backpackers will either camp here or continue on to Blacklock Point. The footworn trail is the best chance to exit from the beach before Blacklock Point because of the high cliffs terminating at a rock that is passable only at low tide (read Hike 44).

Climb the sandbank and find an abandoned road paralleling the beach for about ½ mile, then turn inland through Floras Lake State Park (undeveloped). Parallel the Cape Blanco State Airport to the parking area. There is a maze of abandoned roads throughout the state park, none of which is marked. The only recommendation is to follow the one most used. If the road/trail terminates on the airport runway, walk southward alongside the runway to the parking area just beyond the hangar (for access see Hike 44).

Closest motels are southward in Port Orford. Closest campgrounds are northward at Bandon and southward near Humbug Mountain, which is closed during the winter.

Mouth of Fourmile Creek after a heavy rain

In event of storm, the seasoned traveler will take this opportunity to view the thundering surf leaping high in the air on rocky points from a safe viewpoint. A warm motel room can be a place of intense comfort.

44. CAPE BLANCO STATE AIRPORT TO CAPE BLANCO

Distance: 6 miles one way
Hiking time: 6 hours
Time of year: Late spring to early fall
Tide: Low
Obstacles: River crossing
Maps: Cape Blanco (USGS)
      Curry County #1
      (Oregon Dept. of Transportation)

Read the Southern Oregon Coast Warning in the introduction, "What You'll Need to Know."

This day's hike crosses a grass-covered headland, traverses sandy beaches and a few rock-strewn ones, and crosses a river. This is a beautiful day's hike with picturesque offshore rocks. The hike must be started on a low tide.

From Bandon, drive south on U.S. 101 – past the communities of Langlois and Denmark – to the Cape Blanco State Airport road. Turn right (west). The road is well signed, but there is little warning from the north. It lies a few hundred feet beyond a tourist attraction called "Stone Age Park," across from the South Pacific High School. Don't confuse it with the Cape Blanco Junction to the south. Follow the county road 2½ miles to the entrance to the airport; turn into a graveled parking area. Adjacent to the airport entrance is a sturdy white gate made of steel highway guards. This is the start of the beach hike. The trip ends at Cape Blanco (see Hike 46 for instructions).

The way to the beach follows abandoned roads through Floras Lake State Park (undeveloped). There is a maze of such roads throughout the park. None of the intersections is marked, so finding the right one takes a bit of luck. For the first ½ mile the way parallels the airport. From then on, it is best to follow the road with the most footprints, generally keeping to the right at intersections. During rainy periods the road contains numerous lake-sized mud puddles, which make hiking difficult. After wandering through dense brush for one mile, the road abruptly breaks out on a bluff overlooking the ocean. Follow the road north a short distance and drop down a distinct nose to the beach, about 1½ miles from the car.

On the beach hike southward under impassable cliffs until you reach a

Blacklock Point

battleship bow of rock with an attractive waterfall. In strong north winds the waterfall dissolves in mist. This point can be rounded only at low, low tide over slippery, slimy, seaweed-covered rocks. (An alternate route is described in Hike 45.) After rounding the point, stay close to the cliffs to keep off the slippery rocks as much as possible. A rocky pocket beach shows a possible escape route up a steep, gravelly hillside. Next, round another tiny point with another gravelly beach.

When the way is blocked by a high grass-covered point with a small, sandy beach, walk up a V-shaped valley that usually contains a small stream. Then climb up the steep, grassy slopes to the top of Blacklock Point, with views out over the ocean and south to Cape Blanco. There are nice campsites protected by trees.

From the point, drop down the grassy slope to a sandy beach. In 2 miles, just opposite Castle Rock, you reach the broad delta of Sixes River. The river usually dams up during the summer, when there may be only a small trickle of water. However, it can be 300 feet across and 10 feet deep after a winter storm drops several inches of water. If the river cannot be crossed safely, don't try. Go back to your car and drive to a different beach.

After crossing Sixes River, follow the beach another 1½ miles on cobblestone rocks to Cape Blanco. The easiest way up is via a trail at the low point east of the lighthouse. To reach the state park campground, walk east on the road ½ mile to a junction and then follow signs another ½ mile.

Cape Blanco is the most westerly point in Oregon. The cape is well known for its classic white lighthouse, which is now automated and closed to the public. Perhaps if the lighthouse had been there in 1884, the men aboard the steamer *Alaskan* would have been saved (see Hike 46).

45. BLACKLOCK POINT TRAIL

Distance: 5 miles round trip
Hiking time: 2½ hours
Time of year: Any
Tide: Any (extreme low tide around Battleship Bow Rock)
Obstacles: Difficult route to follow
Map: Curry County #1
      (Oregon Dept. of Transportation)

This is an undeveloped park with beautiful cliffs, a waterfall, offshore rocks, a grass-covered headland, and one of the best chances for solitude on the Oregon coast. It's a place to see wildlife: bobcat, rabbit, deer, a great horned owl; and to see wildflowers: acres of rhododendron, Labrador tea, marsh plants, and irises growing in grassy meadows.

To reach Blacklock Point, drive to Cape Blanco State Airport (formerly Curry County Airport) as described in Hike 44. Walk along the dirt road beyond the steel highway guards. The road parallels the highway for the first mile. Don't take the first right fork, which leads back to the airport. In 300 feet, follow the left fork, an alternate route for beach hikers to Blacklock Point. In ⅛ mile, at a major junction, follow the more heavily traveled trail to the left. The road now swings in a southerly direction, parallel to the ocean. In ⅛ mile, you'll reach a junction with a road to the right. Turn right at this point (a silver snag stands on the left). Past a bare patch of sand, the road narrows into a trail and continues westward down a distinct dip. Beyond are some windfall logs across the trail. Continue down past the windfalls, through deciduous trees, for approximately ⅛ mile. The trail terminates just behind the small stand of conifers at the top of Blacklock Point. The triangular expanse of grass beyond is an excellent place to camp. Cape Blanco looms magnificently to the south. To the north, in the adjacent small valley, is a stream.

It's possible to make this a loop trip by going northward and rounding Battleship Bow Rock at extreme low tide. The small stream flowing over the rock frequently dissipates into mist when the wind blows. Continuing on to the cliff, retrace your steps as indicated in Hikes 43 and 44.

Blacklock Point

Experienced hikers can use a compass to follow game trails to the top of Battleship Bow Rock and a great view to the north. The stream flows over the rock and rises in mist on the wings of the wind. For safety, stay back from the cliff edge.

Battleship Bow at Blacklock Point

46. CAPE BLANCO

Distance: 2½ miles round trip to Blacklock Point
             3 miles round trip to Elk River
Hiking time: 2 hours each
Time of year: Any
Tide: Any
Obstacles: None
Map: Curry County #1
     (Oregon Dept. of Transportation)

A historic farm to explore, two short round-trip beach hikes, and a handsome lighthouse all make this trip memorable. The cape was named "Cape Orford" by Captain George Vancouver on April 24, 1792, but its original Spanish name – Cape Blanco (White) – prevailed.

Three miles north of Port Orford, turn west on the well-marked Cape Blanco Road. After several miles, the road dips down to meadows and old barns near the Sixes River. The next ½ mile floods during intense storms. As the road rises up the next hill, a fork to the right leads to a handsome farmhouse built by the original settler, who created a large dairy and sheep ranch. The farmhouse, now a state park headquarters, is open to the public. Across the meadowland, by the Sixes River, rises another Victorian house. It was built by the original settler's son and is privately owned. Continuing on the road through trees, a turn to the left leads one into a highly developed state camping area, complete with electricity, pavement, and running water, as well as a dumping station. Leave your car in the camping area parking lot. Straight ahead, toward the ocean, is the beginning of the first hike. The terrain narrows into a neck and then rises to the magnificent Cape Blanco Lighthouse. Closed to the public, the automated light is tended by a single Coast Guardsman. From the neck, a scramble trail to the north heads down to the beach and leads to the Sixes River, which may well be dammed at this point. Beyond, up over grassy meadows, is Blacklock Point, a good destination and a view point from which to photograph the lighthouse before returning.

The second hike follows a well-developed trail from the campground southward to the beach. (Here one of our party was caught by the driftwood logs and surging tide during a storm, and fortunately was unhurt.) It's 2½ miles along the beach to the Elk River and back. This is the first leg of Hike 47.

Cape Blanco Lighthouse

The side-wheeler steamer *Alaskan* was lost with 31 lives in this vicinity in 1884. The waves demolished the port guard and loosened the aft house, which began to break up, allowing seas to flood the interior of the vessel. Fortunately it did not have a full complement of passengers, and three lifeboats were successfully launched. The elderly veteran steward refused to leave... and go down with the ship he did. The chief engineer and the second officer, as well as the captain, remained aboard. Captain Howes leaped clear just as the vessel was being sucked down. He and the chief engineer perched on a piece of wreckage. After three hours of searching by the tug *Vigilant*, only Captain Howes and three survivors were picked up. The following morning the *Alaskan's* first officer was sighted from the tug's masthead, clinging to a piece of wreckage that was barely buoyant enough to keep him afloat. The second lifeboat, containing ten men, came ashore at Siuslaw (now called Florence), but all the other boats foundered in the heavy seas, drowning their occupants.

---

47. CAPE BLANCO TO PORT ORFORD

Distance: 7 miles one way
Hiking time: 3 ½ hours
Time of year: Late spring to early fall
Tide: Medium or low
Obstacles: One river and one stream crossing
Maps: Cape Blanco and Port Orford (USGS)
      Curry County #1
      (Oregon Dept. of Transportation)

Read the Southern Oregon Coast Warning in the introduction, "What You'll Need to Know."

This hike, mostly on sand, features a creek and river crossing that could be impossible during the winter months. The way is exposed to the full blast of a southern storm. Sometimes, winds blow up and over Cape Blanco like a horizontal stream of airblown water and foam.

Drive south from Bandon on U.S. 101 past the Sixes River bridge. Just 3 miles short of Port Orford, turn west on the well-marked Cape Blanco Road. Drive 5 ½ miles to about ½ mile short of the lighthouse and find a parking place. The hike will end near Port Orford at a legal access at the end of the Paradise Point Road, which joins U.S. 101 just 500 feet north of the Port Orford city limits.

The hike starts at the lowest point of Cape Blanco, on the neck of land reaching out to the lighthouse. Drop down the south side, cross the driftwood logs, and walk onto the cobblestone beach. In ½ mile you reach a bluff that can only be rounded at medium or low tides. (If the tide is in, a detour is possi-

Cape Blanco, Humbug Mountain in distance

Port Orford

ble. Climb to the state park campground and walk past it to a steep asphalt-covered road leading down to the beach. It is no longer possible to drive onto the beach from here, but the carcass of a truck frame of unknown make shows that it once was.)

Beyond the bluff, the next 2½ miles are on a sandy beach below a long, fluted bluff to the delta of the Elk River and a nice campsite. Here is an interesting phenomenon: the course of the river has moved northward a full mile from that shown on the Curry County map. A massive storm must have driven the sand northward, closing off the river entry and diverting it into the old channel it now occupies. Heavy runoff sometime in the future may change the course back to what is shown on the map.

The large river delta area is used extensively for sheep ranching. Be sure to boil the water. The rusty red roof of a barn is visible on the approaching fluted bluff. No homes are visible. It's 3 miles from the river to the Paradise Point exit. Ahead, Nellie Point is visible. Look sharply for a chimney and a sign indicating Paradise Point. If a modernistic house with the roof anchored down by cables appears on the left, you've missed the beach access, which is located immediately to the north and behind the house. There will probably be people on the beach and certainly footprints. Follow the footprints to the road's end.

A backpacker might want to continue another mile to the end of the walkable beach. It is necessary to wade the outlet creek of Garrison Lake. (This may require waiting for low tide.) Near the end of the beach, follow a cat track up to the city street. (This exit was possible in 1982, but may be blocked by future home building.) Follow the city street eastward to the intersection with U.S. 101. The bus stop is on the northwest corner.

There are motels in Port Orford and camping to the south at Humbug Mountain, which unfortunately is closed in winter.

For access to the southern end of this hike, a sign on U.S. 101, just north of Port Orford, points to Paradise Point.

If the hike is extended, turn west in Port Orford to the Garrison Lake boat launch. Access to the beach is 1½ blocks to the south over city streets and the cat track.

Boat launching at Port Orford

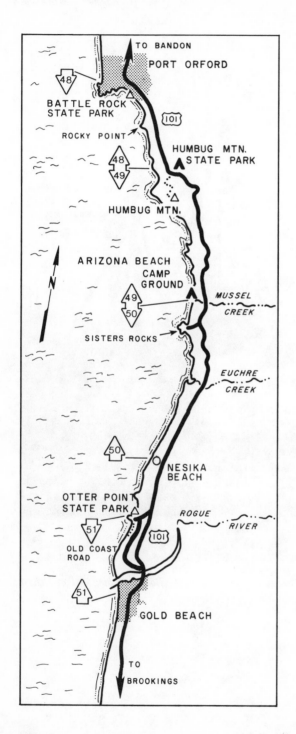

SECTION I.
Port Orford to Gold Beach

Port Orford is a handsome small town with over 130 years of history. It also boasts an unusual fishing pier onto which commercial fishing boats are hoisted by huge derricks. In season it might be possible to buy a fresh crab. For replenishing supplies, Port Orford also offers several well-stocked stores.

Port Orford is located just to the southeast of a large outcropping called "The Head." On the top of "The Head" are a Coast Guard station and a lookout. To the west lies Klooqueh Rock; to the south, Tichenor Rock. The most southerly extension is Nellie's Point. The commercial jetty is located on Graveyard Point.

The original townsite of Port Orford was originally called Ewing Harbor, after the U.S. Coastal Survey vessel *Ewing*, but the name Port Orford persisted. Captain William Tichenor, of the ship *Sea Gull*, landed nine men on June 9, 1851, to commence settlement. The next day they were attacked by the local Indians, who were already at war over the settlement at Gold Beach, to the south, and the resulting loss of their lands. The men retreated onto tiny Battle Rock and ultimately escaped to Umpqua settlement, now Reedsport, 65 miles to the north. This retreat required that they cross the Coquille River at Bandon, as well as Coos Bay and the Coos River.

On July 4, 1851, Captain Tichenor returned with a well-armed party of 67 and established a blockhouse. On September 14, Lieutenant P. T. Wyman, Company I, First Artillery Department of the Pacific, established the most westerly fort on the continental mainland. Fifteen buildings were completed by the spring of 1856. The fort consisted of plank walls reinforced with dirt. The fort was closed in 1856 and the troops were moved to Fort Umpqua; now the site is commemorated by a sign. After his retirement, Captain Tichenor settled in the village, where he lived out his life.

The first section of beach south of Port Orford, much of it rocky, stretches in an arc pierced in the middle by impassable Rocky Point. The beach terminates at the steep cliffs of Humbug Mountain. From there to Nesika Beach, access is intermittent, although U.S. 101 provides magnificent overlooks. Nesika Beach offers excellent low-relief hiking. South of Nesika Beach is a brief gap, impassable along the water's edge. Then comes excellent hiking to the Rogue River at the old community of Gold Beach. (If you wish to further explore the Rogue River area, refer to Hikes 63, 64, and 65.)

Humbug Mountain from Port Orford

48. PORT ORFORD TO HUMBUG MOUNTAIN STATE PARK

Distance: 5 miles one way
Hiking time: 3 to 4 hours
Time of year: All, but best in summer
Tide: Medium to low
Obstacles: Tidal problems and headlands to cross
Map: Curry County #1
　　　(Oregon Dept. of Transportation)

This day's hike is a mixture of sandy beaches, cobblestones, and a few impassable sections where one must retreat to the road and drive. The beach is only walkable at medium to low tide, but of course the road is always drivable, with equally good or better views.

At Battle Rock State Park, drop a few feet to the beach and head south below house-studded bluffs and past many offshore rocks. In ½ mile, cross a stream on driftwood. There is a road access trail at this point. The next 2 miles are a mixture of sand, rock shelves, and cobblestones, where people, with some success, pan for gold. The beach ends 2½ miles from Port Orford at Rocky Point. Retrace your steps 500 feet to a trail leading to the highway and parking area (1¾ miles south of the city).

Just south of Rocky Point there is another access to the beach. Most folks will prefer not to descend here, because the beach is very rocky and is passable only during low tides and moderate surf. A second exit, about ⅛ mile on, starts with a jeep road and ends in a 30-foot slide and scramble onto the beach. The seasoned traveler will retreat if the surf runs up to the rocky point and will keep an eye out to make certain that the tide does not sneak in behind. Continue on the cobblestones around Cole Point until the 1,000-foot cliffs of Humbug Mountain are reached. From here, foot access to Humbug

Battle Rock State Park

Sword fern

Mountain State Park is below a curved bridge. Unfortunately, this very attractive state park, with its grassy campsites and hook-ups, is closed in the winter. The closest motel to the south behind Humbug Mountain likewise may be closed in winter. There are excellent motels in Port Orford.

49. HUMBUG MOUNTAIN

Distance: 6 miles one way
Hiking time: 3½ hours
Time of year: Any
Tide: Any
Obstacles: Gain and loss of 1,700 feet
Map: Curry County #1
     (Oregon Dept. of Transportation)

For a change of pace, climb on a forested trail to the top of 1756-foot Humbug Mountain. The lovely forest makes the trip well worthwhile, which is fortunate because the view from the top is limited. Late May, when the rhododendrons are blooming, is a great time to make this trip.

From Humbug Mountain State Park campground, walk through an underpass below U.S. 101 (past a parking lot south of the highway) and find the Humbug Mountain trail. Switchback steeply upward for 3 miles to the top. At the beginning, the trail is surrounded by a carpet of oxalis and ferns under an umbrella of moss-covered maples, tall evergreen trees, and pleasant-smelling California laurel, which is better known in this neck of the woods as Oregon myrtle.

The first mile remains steep, but afterward the ascent moderates. Most of the way is in forest, with an occasional glimpse through the trees. The consolation is a cool, shaded trail on an otherwise dry hillside. The trail switchbacks upward past 5-foot-thick fir trees and rhododendron bushes up to 15 or 20 feet tall.

The trail ends in a small, grassy meadow with a view south to Nesika Beach.

The descent offers a good opportunity to study the variation in vegetation between the ocean exposure and the sheltered back side of the mountain. The ocean slope tends to favor heavy brush such as salal and slide alder, which make travel extremely slow. As you enter the coniferous margin of the sheltered side of the mountain, the umbrella of mature firs, hemlocks, and pines shuts light out. Salal dwindles in size and density; slide alder exists only in stream gullies. There is almost a total lack of low vegetation except for plentiful moss and small flowers in season. Here traveling is easier. The seasoned wilderness hiker on a cross-country trip will always endeavor to travel under big trees to avoid the clutching fingers of brush.

From Humbug Mountain to Arizona Beach the highway winds along a singing river. Drive slowly. The road tops out in a steep, brown field, with a small overlook with magnificent views. To the north is Humbug Mountain, with its south shoulder – a long ridge of meadows that beckons to the mountaineer. We have not described this route because the ridge terminates in a steep gully, with access off through a fenced meadow leased out to others by absentee landowners. Below the steep ridge to the north extends a rocky beach of several miles. While the beach is accessible, we do not recommend the hike down. It would be slow, rocky going, and would require a return before high tide. The crew of a shipwrecked fishing vessel endeavored to climb over the ridge without success and ultimately exited at the highway.

At 6 miles, U.S. 101 drops down to Arizona Beach and Mussel Creek. You can reach the comfortable-looking commercial campground on the right by turning left into the small motel. A road leads under the highway to the beach. There is also a motel back along the highway in the shadow of Humbug Mountain; other motels are to the south at Gold Beach.

Humbug Mountain trail

American bittern near Arizona Beach

50. ARIZONA BEACH TO NESIKA BEACH

Distance: 9 miles one way
Hiking time: 5 hours
Time of year: Any
Tide: Low
Obstacles: One major stream crossing
Map: Curry County #1
      (Oregon Dept. of Transportation)

This hike must be started at low tide to enable the traveler to slip around some points at low tide. Also on this route are Sisters Rock, a return to the

Beach near Ophir Wayside

highway with a striking view of Nesika Beach, and finally, a beautiful, but somewhat slow beach hike.

As of 1983, access to Arizona Beach is through a private campground. If you wish to park your car, the owner charges the same rate as for camping. If your driver drops you off at the campground and parks the car elsewhere, the fee is less. The campground is attractive but without much development.

Hike southward during medium to low tide. Rounding a corner, you'll come upon sea arches and sandpipers and probably several scramble-overs, if the tide is not completely out. Sisters Rock appears after 1 ½ miles. It is hard to conceive that engineers would make a rock quarry out of such a beautiful headland, but blast they did, with complete indifference to nature. At least the quarry provides a steep access road out. Below and to the south, the dedicated hiker will find a short, round-trip beach. The hike could be terminated at this point.

As you proceed southward on U.S. 101 ½ mile past a large rock, the breath-taking sweep of Nesika Beach comes into view. Park here. No easy access to the beach is visible. A house ahead tempts one to trespass, but don't. Instead, push down through the brush after the terrain eases off. The brief struggle will be worth the lovely 7-mile hike ahead.

Euchre Creek flows across the beach. If it is too high to wade it may be easily crossed on a bridge over U.S. 101. A distinctive-looking building about halfway down the beach is a public information center with drinking water and restrooms. Above are wooded hills and an occasional green-brown field with a few homes. When the beach terminates at a distinctive low head, turn upward on a scramble trail to a road end.

Nesika Beach is a tiny residential community with a general store and a private RV park where tent camping is possible. The closest motels are in Gold Beach. To reach the end of the hike, just south of the RV park, turn right a short block past some small homes. A chain-link fence with a prohibition against trespassing will be on the left side.

Sisters Rock

51. OTTER POINT TO THE ROGUE RIVER

Distance: 4 miles one way
Hiking time: 2 hours
Time of year: Any
Tide: Any
Obstacles: Route difficult to find at the start; must bring water
Map: Curry County #1
    (Oregon Dept. of Transportation)

From Otter Point you can see the long, curving, sandy beach you are about to hike. From here, the beach is tantalizingly inaccessible.

Drive U.S. 101 a couple of miles south of the community of Nesika Beach to the paved but narrow Old Coast Road. Turn right (west) and in another ¼ mile, turn right again on a gravel road, which leads in ⅛ mile to undeveloped Otter Point State Park. Here, a trail to the beach gives the only

Otter Point

legal access to a rugged mile of cobblestones reaching northward to an impassable head. With no exit out except over private property, the hiker has to return to Otter Point ahead of the tide.

To the south is an excellent view of the main route—the long, curving beach that rounds a point and terminates at the Rogue River. Unfortunately, there is no safe descent at this point. Return to the little-used Old Coast Road and walk southward an additional ¾ mile. Here a brush-covered scramble trail descends to the beach. You'll find the trail 200 feet beyond a "One Lane Road" sign, just past the bottom of a dip in the road. (Park here if you want to eliminate road walking.) If you miss the scramble trail, it's only ¼ mile farther to a well-signed beach trail. Here a corridor has been cleaved through the vegetation to the beach.

At the beach, you can turn northward to hike back under the beautiful sandstone cliffs of Otter Point ¾ mile to the north. Southward is a wide, sandy beach. The way first passes under sandstone cliffs, which eventually give way to grassy hills and attractive houses on the low-curving headland of the tiny community of Rogue. The Rogue River lies just ahead, lined by a north jetty where it enters the Pacific.

Another ¾ mile takes you past some attractive condominiums to a classic, arched Oregon-style bridge over which U.S. 101 passes into the county seat of Curry County, the thriving community of Gold Beach.

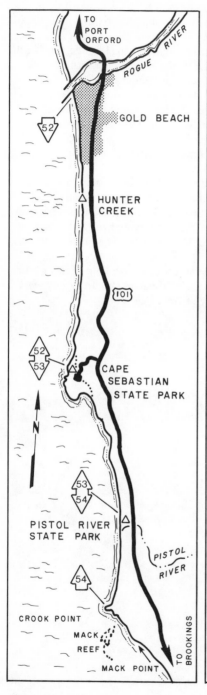
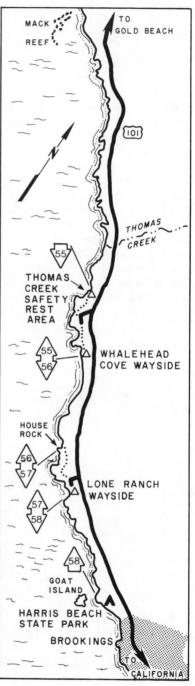

SECTION J.
Gold Beach to Brookings

Gold Beach, the county seat of Curry County, is rich in history and places of interest. Hikers can follow the entire beach around the town, past the airport (where the private pilot had better know crosswind landing techniques), and on into the shadows of Cape Sebastian—unfortunately a dead end.

From the top of the cape a series of trails leads back to the beach and on to Pistol River. After the Thomas Creek bridge there begins a series of short trails that lead up over House Rock and down into Lone Ranch Day Center. Beyond is a short beach hike that leads you to Brookings by way of delightful Harris Beach State Park.

The discovery of gold at the mouth of the Rogue River in the early 1800s brought an influx of miners. Displaced Indians commenced warfare for their tribal lands in 1855 and 1856. Similar skirmishes took place at Port Orford and at Pistol River. Eventually, four small settlements—Whalesburg, Sebastapol, Parrallsville, and Ellensburg—were combined and renamed Gold Beach in 1890. The city has been the seat of Curry County since 1859. A wagon road connected the town to civilization in 1890, and with the opening of a bridge in 1932, U.S. 101 tied the city firmly to the outside world. Gold Beach, however, was not incorporated until 1945.

An interesting fountain in front of the Curry County Courthouse in Gold Beach is dedicated to "Bullhide Moore." Bullhide, one of the early pioneers, operated a general store and a slaughterhouse (the source of his name), and also ran sheep on the hills to the west of town. His general store was on the west side of the street and faced the courthouse and hills to the east. Bullhide was probably the first unofficial animal control officer. He kept a rifle in his store, and, when he saw a dog after his sheep, he would simply step to the door of his store and deter any canine aggressiveness. Bullhide was, in addition, a strong moral and political figure in the town. After his death, in the late 1960s at a very great age, his seven daughters wished to place a statue of him in front of the county courthouse. Not all residents agreed; the compromise was the fountain.

Halfway through town, alongside the fairground, is a fine museum. Gold Beach and other coastal Oregon towns have a very strong feeling of history and the independent development and settlement of the region. The photographs displayed in the museum date back to the late 1800s. The museum also owns the vessel *Mary D. Hume*, which is located at the east end of the

Mary D. Hume *moored at Gold Beach*

boat basin in the Rogue River, quite close to the bridge. The *Mary D. Hume*, built in Gold Beach in 1880, was named after the builder's wife. The ship did service originally as a coastal schooner between Gold Beach and San Francisco and as far north as Seattle. Unfortunately, the bar at the river entrance allowed the vessel to enter and leave only in good weather.

Eventually, as a whaler, the *Mary D. Hume* sailed to Alaska, where it was stuck in ice through several Nome winters. It returned with a huge cargo of whale baleen. In 1914 it was converted to a tug. Crowley Marine Company retired the vessel in 1977, and returned it to Gold Beach. In 1979 the ship was placed on the national registry. As of 1983 it's not open, but people of Gold Beach are going through the voluminous paperwork necessary for its restoration.

52. GOLD BEACH TO CAPE SEBASTIAN

Distance: 3 miles one way to Hunter Creek
     8 miles round trip from Hunter Creek to Cape Sebastian
Hiking time: 2 hours 1 way; 4 hours round trip
Time of year: Any
Tide: Any
Obstacles: None
Map: Curry County #1
     (Oregon Dept. of Transportation)

This hike starts near a windswept airport and proceeds past a small town, which seems surprisingly remote from this easy-to-walk 3-mile-long beach.

View from Cape Sebastian

Beyond Hunter Creek, a wonderful round-trip wilderness hike beckons the wanderer. It ends beneath magnificent Cape Sebastian. Only a few houses mark the landscape, and there is a small stream beside which to camp.

After crossing the bridge over the Rogue River into Gold Beach, turn right. Go past the boat basin, follow the gravel road to the south jetty, and park. The airport is immediately to the left, with the town behind it. You may be rewarded by the sight of a light plane crabbing into a crosswind for a touch and go on the strip. Because of the low terrain, the town is set back from the beach margins.

At 3 miles, having passed the town, the hiker reaches Hunter Creek. If the water is too high for wading, follow the easy access to U.S. 101 and return to the beach on the south side of the creek. There's a parking area at Hunter Creek that serves as an alternate beginning to the hike.

A large monolith several hundred feet high can be passed at medium tide via the beach and at high tide via the nearby highway. Beyond is a beautiful, smooth, 4-mile-long beach terminating beneath the forested shoulders of the granitic upthrust of Cape Sebastian. The dense undergrowth deters any thought of continuing. The road ascending from this point to the highway is on private property. At the highway, it is blocked by a gate clearly marked "Private Property, No Trespassing." Perhaps in the future the road will be open to public use, as homes are constructed near the beach.

Shortly before Cape Sebastian there is a nice campsite by a trickling stream, with only a few, probably empty, houses above. So the return to Gold Beach or the Hunter Creek parking area can be delayed until the following day.

53. CAPE SEBASTIAN TO PISTOL RIVER

Distance: 5 miles one way
Hiking time: 2½ hours
Time of year: Any
Tide: Any
Obstacles: None
Map: Curry County #1
    (Oregon Dept. of Transportation)

South of Gold Beach and Hunter Creek, U.S. 101 rises dramatically – in a series of sweeping turns with great overlooks – to a crest behind Cape Sebastian. A turn to the right to the state park leads up a hill too steep for trailers and narrow at the top. It leads to one of the most spectacular overlooks on the Oregon coast. Southward lie the great white crescent beaches of the Pistol River, with Mack Arch beyond. To the north a great crescent of sand stretches to Gold Beach.

A paved trail with benches leads westerly to the crest. The trail soon pops into a tunnel of trees with an occasional wild iris and other flowers in season. The trail now switchbacks down the nose of the cape to the rocks at its foot. Here are curious sandstone rocks filled with holes where a softer conglomerate has eroded out. The trail continues on around the rocks and to the south. After some rising and falling it drops onto the Pistol River beach, which is visible from above. The highway descends shortly to parallel the fine ocean beach. The Pistol River beach is reached at Hunters Cove, and Hunters Island lies to the left offshore. It is 3½ miles to this point.

The mouth of the Pistol River was the scene of a famous battle in 1856 when the Rogue River Indians besieged 34 volunteers in a rough stockade at this point. The Indians fought with savage fury and repeatedly charged. Hand-to-hand combat was carried on for several days. The Indians were finally

Cape Sebastian

Natural Bridge

dispersed by regular troops arriving under the command of Captains Ord and Jones.

Cape Sebastian was named by the Spanish explorer Sebastian Biziana in 1603.

54. PISTOL RIVER TO CROOK POINT

Distance: 4 miles round trip
Hiking time: 2½ hours
Time of year: Any
Tide: Any
Obstacles: Brush to walk through
Map: Curry County #1
      (Oregon Dept. of Transportation)

Mack Arch, with its curious hole, can be seen easily from the top of Cape Sebastian, but a closer view is surprisingly difficult. There is no public access by road to Crook Point, contrary to indications on the map.

Immediately south of the Pistol River bridge, a short road leads down onto the beach through a state day park. Beyond is an excellent hiking beach that leads in 2 miles to Crook Point. The point can't be rounded at beach level. A scramble to the rocks at the top leads one to vegetation. Mack Arch, with its curious hole, and Mack Reef, as well as Saddle Rocks, are immediately to the south. Some careful travel on the edge of the brush is now in order. The traveler may wonder whether the view is worth the effort.

It would be a serious mistake to turn inland here in an attempt to round the point. A retreat back down the beach to Pistol River is appropriate.

Hunters Cove

Mouth of Pistol River

Arch Rock near Thomas Creek Safety Rest Area

55. THOMAS CREEK TO WHALE HEAD COVE

Distance: 4 miles
Hiking time: 2½ hours
Time of year: Any
Tide: Any
Obstacles: Steep hillsides
Map: Curry County #1
    (Oregon Dept. of Transportation)

This is a series of three short, close-together, spectacular trail trips, each looping outward and returning to U.S. 101.

From the Thomas Creek Safety Rest Area, 20 miles south of Gold Beach, descend the trail ⅛ mile, turning left at the junction along the way. A view to the north reveals the high stanchions of the Thomas Creek bridge, reputedly the highest in the state. Wandering through the trees, the trail comes out on a

View from Indian Sands trail

Beach strawberry

spectacular steep hillside with the surf far below. Walk carefully. From here the trail climbs back to U.S. 101.

For the next hike, it is necessary to walk ⅛ mile south along the highway past an impossible chasm with a wind fence. If you choose to do so, please watch for traffic. The trail begins just to the north of the crest. After several switchbacks, it goes through a small valley and traverses outward and downward spectacularly around a nose just above the sea. Some sheep may be browsing in the meadows. They seem to keep these trails passable. After rounding a corner "Indian Sands" appears. It is a large, windblown series of sand dunes spilling down the hillside to just above the ocean, where they terminate in small cliffs. The indistinct route lies upward and to the south just below the trees and vegetation. To find the trail will probably require some searching. The trail now continues on, again around the corner, again termi-

Wild iris

nating at U.S. 101. A steep, wide trail leads out of the south end of the Indian Sands viewpoint parking lot to intersect this route.

For the final short hike, it is again necessary to walk south along U.S. 101 ⅛ mile, past an impossible crevasse until the cut of the trail across the hillside is clearly visible from the road. Or you may prefer to drive south to the Whale Head Cove Wayside and begin the hike from there. The trail proceeds through brush and trees, offering spectacular vistas from cliffs above crashing surf. It rounds a corner and returns to U.S. 101 at the Whale Head Cove Wayside. Follow the trail carefully. A shortcut leads to a rather steep sandbank. Don't attempt to cross this, because a fall could cause injury.

The nearest motels are at Brookings to the south, with excellent camping at Harris Beach State Park. There is possible beach camping beyond Whale Head Cove.

Whale Head Cove

56. WHALE HEAD COVE TO HOUSE ROCK

Distance: 3 miles one way
Hiking time: 2 hours
Time of year: Any
Tide: Any, but better at low tide
Obstacles: 50-foot elevation gain; indistinct start of trail
Map: Curry County #1
     (Oregon Dept. of Transportation)

Follow this trail over sandy beach, across grassy meadows, and into forest, until you reach a spectacular view.

A rather steep road descends to the public restrooms and picnic area of Whale Head Cove, with Whale Head Island just offshore. Cross the stream by wading or on the logs, and proceed southward over excellent beach for 1 ½ miles. At ½ mile, a trail descends from the left from another overlook. Wooded terrain rises steeply to the left, and ahead, jutting into the horizon, is House Rock. The beach ends by a steep, grassy meadow, which you ascend southward. The slash of the trail becomes visible ahead as it crosses a steep face. After gaining the trail, follow a brief traverse. The trail then switchbacks very steeply up the nose of a ridge through grass and brush. After a gain of approximately 400 feet, it plunges around a corner, downward, and into mixed deciduous and coniferous trees. Continuing to climb and improve, the trail breaks out of forest at the sweeping 360° view from House Rock. Northward is Humbug Mountain and to the south is Brookings.

Beach camping is possible well south of the day area, but boil the water. There are excellent camping spots and excellent motels at Brookings, 5 miles to the south.

---

57. HOUSE ROCK TO LONE RANCH WAYSIDE

Distance: 2 to 3 miles one way
Hiking time: 1½ to 2 hours
Time of year: Any
Tide: Any
Obstacles: Steep, sandy bank; must bring water
Map: Curry County #1
  (Oregon Dept. of Transportation)

This is a trail hike with an option of wandering through meadows or taking a side trip to a pocket beach.

The trail starts in the parking lot immediately south of the memorial at

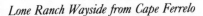
Lone Ranch Wayside from Cape Ferrelo

House Rock Wayside. The trail goes down rather steeply to a fork on the right. For a side trip, follow the fork to a steep, sandy bank, down which you can scramble onto a half-mile pocket beach. Back at the fork, the main trail enters a ravine in the woods. After crossing a bridge, the trail switchbacks up to Cape Ferrelo Wayside parking area. The trail continues out the far side of the parking area and descends through grassy meadows to Lone Ranch Wayside, with restrooms, picnic areas, and fresh water.

An alternate hike would be to drop onto the pocket beach noted above. Turn southward, and then wander over the grassy meadows of Cape Ferrelo and over easy, gentle terrain down into the Lone Ranch Wayside.

Camping and motels are 4 miles away to the south, at Brookings.

58. LONE RANCH WAYSIDE TO HARRIS BEACH STATE PARK

Distance: 3½ miles one way
Hiking time: 3 to 4 hours
Time of year: Any
Tide: Low
Obstacles: Heavy brush in some places
Map: Curry County #1
     (Oregon Dept. of Transportation)

This walk down a curving beach takes you to an area of jagged rocks, thundering surf, thrilling views, and picturesque islands.

From the Lone Ranch Wayside (restrooms available) there is a pleasant cove to visit and a corner that can be rounded at low tide. It's worth taking the time to explore them on a 1-mile round trip. Unfortunately, the terrain ultimately ends in a rocky cove with no reasonable way out. Instead, return on the meadows just above the beach to the wayside.

Drive U.S. 101 until the next vista of curved beach comes in sight. Brookings is visible in the distance. Immediately past a new condominium development (1983) there is scramble access to the beach. If this is no longer legal, continue down the highway until it's possible to safely drop down the steep rocks to the beach. (Plan to be here at low tide, when you can walk northward to admire the colors and caves of Painted Rock and explore the cove and tide pools just beyond.) Southward, the beach curves invitingly with the road high above. Part way down the beach is an isolated house. At this point, rolling bluffs appear. You may encounter some tidal problems and cobblestones as you round the corner of the bluff. If the tide is in it's possible to climb the bluff, walk through the grass, and drop down into Harris Beach State Park. However, at low tide, you can pass Goat Island Bird Sanctuary and approach the

Harris Beach State Park

handsome Harris Beach day center, where there are restrooms. The entire area abounds in jagged rock "teeth" and thundering surf, with many islands offshore and lovely vistas above.

On top of the bluff, a park astraddle U.S. 101 has electrical hook-ups, isolated camping areas, and a backpacker-biker walk-in camp (little improved, but at $1.00 the price is reasonable). Across the road is the interpretive day center.

From the Harris Beach day center, a curved route of ½ mile over cobblestones, rocks, and sand takes the traveler southward behind the Dragons Teeth toward Brookings. The only way out is over a series of private driveways leading up to three or four houses. Please do not trespass. At the top is a house of striking green with a red roof. Beyond, the beach dissolves in a steep hillside too difficult to warrant climbing. The return trip to the day center affords a vista of the Dragons Teeth rocks and the bird sanctuary offshore. This is an excellent place to investigate tide pools and marine life.

The interpretive center across the road, with its displays, is well worth the short, ½-mile stroll. Watch the traffic as you cross U.S. 101. On the west side of the highway, near the overnight camping area, a paved bike trail invites a walk into the town of Brookings.

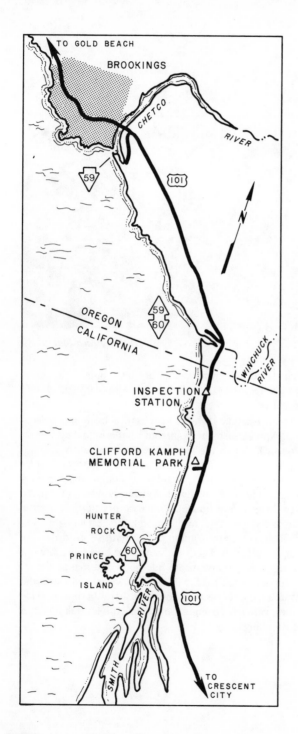

SECTION K.
Brookings to Smith River

The beach hiking at Brookings begins at the south jetty of the Chetco River, where there are real tidal problems, and continues south to the Winchuck River. The next section passes the Oregon-California border on an excellent beach that ends at the Smith River.

The town of Brookings is the regional commercial center of southwestern Oregon. Its economy is based on lumber, fishing, tourism, and use of retirement and vacation homes. The main part of town sits on a bench south of Harris Beach State Park. The city has motels, camping (Harris Beach), medical facilities, grocery shopping, restaurants, and other facilities. The town is divided by the Chetco River, which you cross on the southernmost high bridge on U.S. 101 in Oregon. Immediately south of the bridge and to the right is a shopping center; below is a large, well-developed harbor for the commercial fishing industry – a great place for photography.

Look for the weekly regional newspaper at the newsstands. It gives a flavor of the area and its events and problems.

Fishing fleet at Brookings

59. CHETCO RIVER TO WINCHUCK RIVER

Distance: 5 miles one way
Hiking time: 2½ hours
Time of year: Any
Tide: Low
Obstacles: Three headlands to cross
Map: Curry County #1
     (Oregon Dept. of Transportation)

If the tide is low enough, this next hike can be done entirely on the beach. However, there are three headlands to get around: the first requires a low tide, and the second, a low, low tide. If you can round the second, the third should be easy.

From the Chetco River bridge, turn right at the shopping center and drive past the handsome boat basin on the right and a trailer park on the left. The parking lot here proclaims itself a campground, but it's only suitable for wheeled camping. Leave your car here.

Beginning at extreme low tide, go southward over a good beach under a cliff until you reach a rocky promontory with a keyhole. At a short ⅛ mile, below lovely homes, comes the major obstacle of the trip – another rocky promontory. If this cannot be passed, return. The land above is intensely developed with private homes, the owners of which have obviously endured substantial trespassing and have posted appropriate signs.

Once past these two obstacles, the traveler can continue on a nice beach below handsome homes to a third point, which should offer no difficulty in view of the still-low tide. After that, it's pleasant travel until rounding the point at the Winchuck River. There is a quiet parking lot on the north side of the river just before the U.S. 101 bridge.

An alternate approach to the beach is through an undeveloped state park. From the south jetty in Brookings, go up the road, passing the trailer park on the left, to the first major turn to the right. Follow this lane, which will wander along through a nice residential area of small homes. After approximately 2 miles, the road opens to fields. The state park property (not yet signed) is identifiable by a rather large rock. Two wooden posts mark an opening in the wire fence. A side road through the opening leads directly to the bluff. A scramble trail to the beach allows access to the north past the easy third point to the low, low tide point. The beach to the south can now be traversed without tidal problems.

Motels are in Brookings; camping, at Harris Beach State Park.

Beach south of Brookings

60. WINCHUCK RIVER TO SMITH RIVER

Distance: 5 miles one way
Hiking time: 2½ hours
Time of year: Any
Tide: Any
Obstacles: Small headland at end
Maps: Curry County #1, Crescent County #1
      (both Oregon Dept. of Transportation)

For all practical purposes, the Winchuck River marks the end of the Oregon coast hikes. But across the river, there is still ½ mile of Oregon before crossing the state line into California, and as long as you are walking that far, you might as well go all the way to the Smith River. Besides, the view of Prince Island is well worth the effort.

Mouth of Winchuck River

The few homes at the beginning and end of this nice beach hike do not detract from it. No monument stands at the boundary between Oregon and California.

The hike starts at the parking lot located just north of the Winchuck River bridge. Cross the bridge on the pedestrian sidewalk, and drop down immediately onto the river bank, which leads out to the ocean. Southward, on firm sand, you pass a primitive airstrip and a number of homes. At this point you may encounter people racing by noisily on motorbikes. I strongly believe that beaches should be for people, not wheels.

In one mile, at a rocky corner, the beach runs out. By this time the traveler has passed into California. From here, big rock scrambling is in order for a short stretch. Above the rocks is a handsome house. Dropping back onto the beach, you reach a cliff with a small stream, below a highway bridge. If the stream is swollen with storm water, take a legal-access trail leading up the north bank. Cross the bridge and drop back down through the brush.

Beyond the stream appears a low bank without houses. In the distance, a large green hill rises; underfoot are sandpiper tracks; above, gulls wheel and screech. The beach is usually empty of people.

Ahead is Prince Island. In about 3 miles you pass Clifford Kamph Memorial Park, with its picnic tables, water, and modern restrooms. The trip could end at this point, since there is easy access to U.S. 101, but it's a shame to stop on such a nice beach. So continue on until you reach a point with a few houses above. By staying on the rock and doing a little scrambling, you can stay out of their front yards. Across the mouth of the Smith River is a long inaccessible spit. Upstream ⅛ mile is a parking lot. From U.S. 101 turn right ¾ mile to the parking lot at the sign "Mouth Smith River."

There is an interesting curiosity a short distance farther on U.S. 101 to the south: a large, white passenger ship that appears to be on a collision course with the highway. It's a German-built yacht, now a curiosity shop after service with the U.S. military during World War II.

There are motels in the vicinity, as well as a private campground at this location.

Drift Creek

SECTION L.
Inland Hikes

The following hikes are not along the beach–they're a few miles inland–but are of special interest. Because these hike descriptions are, by and large, invitations to explore regional areas, we have not provided detailed maps but have simply directed you toward a few of the many hikes that are available.

Several of these hikes follow major rivers. The great rivers draining from the interior to the ocean at infrequent places on the Oregon coast afforded early pioneers access to minerals, timber, homesites, and farmlands. Some of the major rivers were historic pioneer routes. The coastal road, U.S. 101, was completed in segments over many years–some as late as the 1930s. Each segment opened with construction over major obstacles, such as Neahkahnie Mountain and Cape Perpetua, or with the construction of handsome, photogenic bridges, such as those over the Rogue and Chetco rivers.

Hike 61, the climb up Saddle Mountain, provides a magnificent view westward to the Seaside area and northward to the Columbia. Colorful wildflowers brighten the landscape in season.

Hike 62 takes you from the vicinity of Waldport to a roadless wilderness forest of fir and hemlock alternating with stands of tall salal and salmonberry.

Hikes 63, 64, and 65 run near the Rogue River, the site of a famous gold strike. Today, tourists can ride the "Mailboat" up the river from Gold Beach and hike back.

In addition, ambitious hikers can follow any number of trails leading from the Brookings area into the Kalmiopsis Wilderness, in the nearby Siskiyou Mountains. In spite of its proximity to the ocean, this area is noted for its dryness and extreme heat during the summer months. Rattlesnakes are common, and poison-oak grows throughout the wilderness, especially in valley bottoms. For trail information, consult local offices of the U.S. Forest Service.

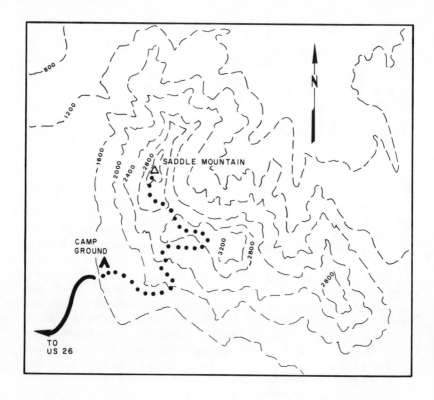

61. SADDLE MOUNTAIN

Distance: 7 miles round trip
Hiking time: 5 hours
Time of year: Best May to November
Obstacles: 1900-foot elevation gain
Map: Saddle Mountain (USGS), but trail does not show

Climb to the top of 3283-foot Saddle Mountain with its two camel-like humps, a landmark visible from Astoria to Seaside. From the top look down on the cities as well as the Columbia River, ships far out on the ocean, and south to Nehalem Bay. The biggest reward is on a clear day, when Mt. Rainier, Mt. St. Helens, Mt. Adams, and Mt. Hood are all visible.

This is not a trail for young children or beginning hikers: the way is steep and at times rough and a bit treacherous. Don't attempt this trail when the exposed cliffs are covered with snow or ice. There is some question whether the trail is 3 or 4 miles long, but, regardless, it will seem like 5 or 6.

From Seaside follow U.S. 101 south about 4 miles and turn left on U.S. 26. Ten miles from this intersection, turn left on the well-signed Saddle Mountain State Park road. It is paved, but only about 1½ cars wide. The road twists and turns like a snake for 7 miles to a tent-only camping area, a parking lot, and the trailhead—elevation about 1500 feet.

The trail is well marked. The first 500 feet, to a water tank, is paved—then it becomes a legitimate trail. The way starts in forest where in May trilliums, yellow wood violets, oxalis, bleeding heart, and some beautiful pink coast fawn lilies are all in bloom.

As the trail switchbacks upward, the forest is interspersed with cliffs that open up views of tree farms and miles of clearcuts. (Depressing as these clearcuts may be, it is far better to be cutting trees here near sea level, where trees mature in 60 to 80 years, than in the Cascades at 3000 to 6000 feet, where they take 100 to 300 years.)

Deer grazing beside Saddle Mountain trail

Summit of Saddle Mountain

After numerous switchbacks, at about 2 miles, the trail reaches the saddle for which the mountain was named. The trail stays close to the ridge top, drops several hundred feet, and then makes the final steep climb over a badly eroded and sometimes exposed area to the top of the 3283-foot north peak. The site of a former fire lookout, the north peak has breathtaking views. The south peak appears to be slightly higher but the map shows it to be 4 feet lower.

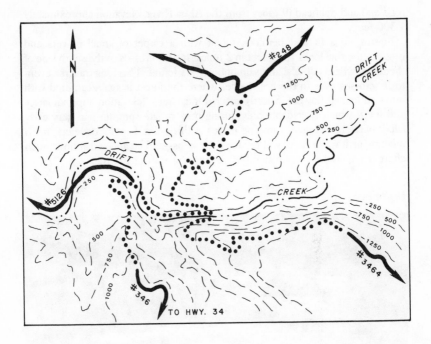

62. DRIFT CREEK TRAILS

Distance: 4 or more miles round trip
Hiking time: 2½ hours or more
Time of year: Summer and fall
Obstacles: Gain and loss of 1,100 feet
Map: Lincoln County #2
      (Oregon Dept. of Transportation)

Accessible by three trails, Drift Creek Valley, a wild pocket in the northern Coast Range, has been set aside as a roadless recreation area. A trail brochure can be obtained from the Supervisor's Office, Siuslaw National Forest, P. O. Box 1148, Corvallis, Oregon, 97330, or from district offices in Waldport, Alsea, or Hebo. The brochure gives directions for finding all three trailheads.

To gain access to the Horse Creek Trailhead South, drive eastward 7 miles from Waldport on Highway 34 to where it crosses the Alsea River. On the north side of the river, turn left onto Risley Creek Road. After a few feet turn right onto Forest Road No. 3446, a narrow paved road with infrequent turn-outs. At 7½ miles, turn left onto Forest Road No. 3464 and continue to the road end and trailhead (9 miles from the Alsea River, elevation approximately 1,300 feet).

Starting in a fir and hemlock forest with a carpet of small flowers and mosses, the trail loses 1,100 feet in 2 miles. It then crosses to the south side of the ridge, where tall salal and salmonberry are found. This long traverse eventually crosses over to the north side, where the forest is again carpeted with moss and small flowers. Shortly reach Drift Creek (elevation approximately 200 feet), which is wadable only during mid- to late summer and very early fall. There are excellent camping places at this point. Careful travelers, upon meeting high water here, will retrace their steps – and be amazed at how much effort is required to regain that 900 feet to the start of the trail.

Drift Creek

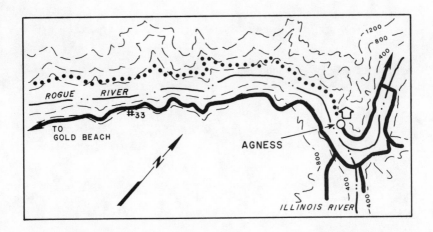

63. ROGUE RIVER BASIN: LOWER ROGUE RIVER TRAIL

Distance: 6 to 24 miles round trip
Hiking time: 3 hours to 3 days
Time of year: Any
Obstacles: None
Map: Curry County #1
   (Oregon Dept. of Transportation)

Early settlers used the Rogue River as their highway to the interior. The gold strikes and mining activities that gave Gold Beach its name caused construction of a 70-mile-long river trail prior to 1887. By the late 1800s, according to the Curry County Commissioner's journal, the trail had become a public highway from Bagnell's Ferry (at Gold Beach) and Mule Creek. By 1919, during the heyday of mining activities, the trail was widened to 4 feet for narrow-gauge carts. But when a county road was built to Agness, the lower trail was abandoned and not reopened until 1976.

In 1978, Congress set aside 84 miles as the "Wild and Scenic Rogue River." Twelve miles of trail along the north bank of the river from Agness to Lobster were reconstructed. The new trail follows the old 4-foot-wide "public highway" as closely as possible; in many places, the old highway bed can be seen.

From the town of Gold Beach, either take one of the tour boats to Agness or drive the road. If you drive, start on the south side of the Rogue River bridge (signed "Jerrys Flat"). Continue 31 miles upstream to a crossing of the Rogue

Rogue River from lower river trail

River and a four-way intersection. Straight ahead is Forest Service Road 33. The right-hand road goes 4 miles to the upper trail. Turn left on the road signed "Agness" and drive 3 miles to an intersection by an abandoned store. Turn right to the Agness Post Office at 3½ miles; the trailhead is directly opposite. There is no space for parking near the post office, so the Forest Service recommends parking ¾ mile up the road near their station.

The first 2½ miles extend across private land and alternate between logging roads and segments of trail. Morris Rodgers Creek is perhaps the best campsite on the hike. As always, the careful traveler will leave no garbage.

At 2¾ miles, the trail enters public land; there's a view here. Three miles along is Painted Rock, an overhang where Indians left messages with colored clay.

The trail stays high above the water, with a windowlike view down through the trees. We recommend the trip at least as far as Painted Rock, although you may travel much farther if you wish.

The tourist lodges at Agness require advance reservations, which can be obtained from tour boat companies or the Chamber of Commerce in Gold Beach.

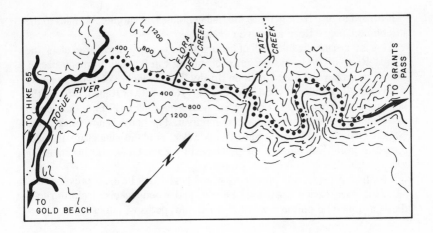

64. ROGUE RIVER BASIN: WILDERNESS TRAIL

Distance: 14 to 80 miles round trip
Hiking time: 1 to 10 days
Time of year: Any
Obstacles: None
Map: Curry County #1
     (Oregon Dept. of Transportation)

This is an exciting hike on an old mining trail. From the south side of the Rogue River bridge at Gold Beach, drive upriver 31 miles on the road marked Jerrys Flat and Agness to a bridge crossing the Rogue. A few feet farther, on the other side of the bridge, is a four-way intersection. Straight ahead the way becomes Forest Service Road 33; the left road goes to Agness. Go right on the Agness-Illahe Road 4 miles to the trailhead at Illahe.

The trail proceeds upriver, seldom on the level, sometimes on top of a cliff high above the river, sometimes at water level. It runs past abandoned farms into cathedrals of old-growth fir trees, through junglelike stands of myrtle, within oak forests, and over steep grassy meadows.

After 2 miles, enter the Wild Rogue Wilderness. At 4¼ miles from the trailhead, pass Flora Dell Creek, with a charming little waterfall and a small, but unfortunately littered, camping area on the beach.

At 6 miles, pass Clay Hill Creek Lodge, and at 7 miles reach Tate Creek Falls, the recommended destination. There are attractive campsites on both sides of the falls.

It is hard to turn back here, as the trail continues on another 33 miles to the Josephine County Road at Grave Creek.

This is a fascinating hike, full of history. Gold was first discovered along the Rogue River in 1851, and evidence of mining can be seen in many places. Only 2 miles beyond Tate Creek on Brushy Bar the ditches of a gold mine are still visible. Ten miles beyond Tate Creek is Rogue River Ranch, built by the first white settlers in 1890. The present house was built in 1903. It first served as a trading post and finally as a vacation retreat. The house is now listed in the National Register of Historic Sites. Winkle Bar, an old mining claim 16 miles upstream from Tate Creek, was purchased by Zane Grey, and his small log cabin is still standing on private property.

This hike provides an opportunity to see large black bears, ospreys, turkey vultures, deer, eagles, great blue herons, and woodpeckers. Unfortunately, there also may be poison ivy, wood ticks, and, perhaps, rattlesnakes.

Rogue River in the Wild Rogue Wilderness

Flora Dell Creek

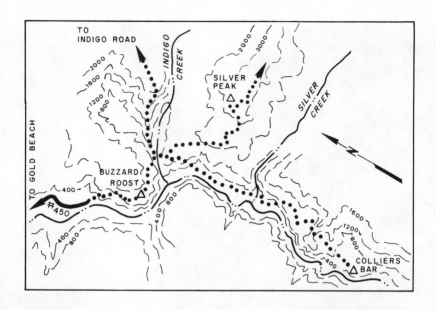

65. ROGUE RIVER BASIN: ILLINOIS RIVER TRAIL

Distance: 8 to 54 miles round trip
Hiking time: 2 to 8 days
Time of year: Any
Obstacles: None
Map: Curry County #1
(Oregon Dept. of Transportation)

The Illinois River, a tributary of the Rogue, has a long history of mining activities.

From Gold Beach, follow the Jerrys Flat and Agness Road 28 miles upstream. Immediately after crossing the high bridge over the Illinois River, turn right on County Road 450 for another 3¼ miles to the Illinois River trailhead (elevation 234 feet).

The hiker will find that the first ½ mile to Nancy Creek has some altitude gain and loss. The next 2 miles rise smartly to 1156-foot Buzzard Roost, which has an excellent overlook. While better views can be gained from the exposed rocks, discretion dictates against climbing them.

From Buzzard Roost, the trail descends 1½ miles to Indigo Creek at 4 miles

Illinois River from Buzzards Roost

and an excellent campsite on private property (the privilege can be revoked).

At Indigo Creek there are four alternatives. First, you may climb 3000 feet up a ridge to Indigo Prairie and a primitive logging road. A second trail leads to 4126-foot Silver Peak, a former fire lookout site. The third and fourth alternatives follow the main trail and at 6 miles reach the Illinois River. After crossing Silver Creek at 8 miles, the trail enters the Kalmiopsis Wilderness. At 8½ miles is a junction where the right trail continues upriver to Colliers Bar, over a 1200-foot pass. The left fork continues for 27 miles to Briggs Creek Road, crossing the Kalmiopsis Wilderness over 3398-foot Little Bald Mountain.

Watch for rattlers and poison oak.

LIST OF HIKES SUITABLE
FOR ROUND TRIPS

While a round trip can be done on any of the beaches, the following make particularly good round-trip day hikes:

5 – Ecola State Park.

9 – Short Sand Beach to Cape Falcon and back.

12 – Round-trip hike on the Nehalem Spit.

14 – Tillamook Spit.

19 – Side-trip hike to Cape Lookout.

20 – Round trip on the Nestucca Bay Spit.

21 – Round trip to Porter Point.

22 – Nature Conservancy Trail. Instead of descending, return to the car.

23 – Round-trip day hike to Harts Cove.

24 – Hike the Gleneden Spit to its end and return to the car.

31 – Any of Cape Perpetua Trails, especially St. Perpetua Trail.

33 – Drive the access to Siltcoos River and explore the area north and south.

35 – Tahkenitch Campground to Threemile Creek and return to the car.

36 – Explore Threemile Lake and hike the spit from Threemile Creek to the Umpqua River and return.

39 – Drive to Horsfall and explore the beach both ways.

40 – Explore Cape Arago.

41 – Explore the Coquille River Lighthouse.

46 – Explore Cape Blanco, especially the hike north to Blacklock Point for a view.

49 – Climb Humbug Mountain.

51 – Explore Otter Point.

52 – From the Cape Sebastian view point, hike an additional ½ mile for the magnificent view to the north.

53 – Explore the two trails, one to the north, one to the south ½ mile each way.

53 – Short round-trip beach hike to the south at low tide and back on the meadows above.

58 – Explore Harris Beach side trip.

Great blue heron

Japanese fishing float in Oregon Dunes National Recreation Area

LIST OF HIKES SUITABLE
FOR BACKPACKING

Because of the high level of development along the Oregon coast, there is little wilderness camping (we have noted campgrounds in each of the individual sections). The following would make good backpacking trips:

9 & 10 – Camp in Short Sand State Park.

13 – Camp in Barview Campground.

32 – Descend onto Hecata Beach and camp at the outfall of Sutton Creek. Continue on to the north jetty of the Siuslaw River.

33 – Hike from Siuslaw River to Siltcoos River and camp in Siltcoos Campground. Continue on to Threemile Creek to camp or continue on to Tenmile Creek. Explore Threemile Lake and exit as indicated in Hike 36.

37 – Hike from the Umpqua River to Tenmile Creek Camp. Continue on to exit at Horsfall (Hike 38).

42 – Hike from Bandon. Go past Fourmile Creek and camp at the little creek below the exit to Cape Blanco State Park. Continue on past Battleship Bow at low tide and camp on the top of Blacklock Point (Hike 45). Continue on to Cape Blanco.

47 – Hike from Cape Blanco to Sixes River and camp. Cross the river and continue on to Port Orford.

Index